INSIGHT Pocket Guides

Discovery CHANNEL

The guidebooks that take the place of a tour guide

PLUS PULLOUT MAP

CORFU

This is the guide that answers the questions you'd ask a friend who lived on Corfu. Which attractions are *really* worth seeing? What excursions shouldn't be missed? Written by Insight's experts on Greece, it is based on intimate knowledge of the island.

Everything you need is in this book:

◆ History and culture
Corfu's past and present explained in a nutshell. *Pages 11–17*

◆ Tailor-made itineraries
17 itineraries covering the island, linking essential sights but also venturing off the beaten track. *Pages 23–67*

◆ Shopping, eating out and nightlife
Insider's tips on what to buy, where to eat and where to stay out late during you[...] *Pages 69–79*

◆ Essential practical information
Hotels, climate, currency, getting aro[...] useful addresses, etc. *Pages 83–96*

◆ Detailed pullout map
This gives an overview of the tours a[...] also be used independently of the gui[...]

www.insightguides.com

By the editors of the award-winning Insight Guides

£7.99

ISBN 981-4120-32-4
00799
9 789814 120326

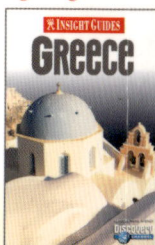

INSIGHT GUIDES
GREECE

KW-054-069

PLUS PULLOUT MAP

INSIGHT POCKET • CORFU

Discovery CHANNEL

INSIGHT POCKET GUIDE

CORFU

Discovery
CHANNEL

APA PUBLICATIONS L
Part of the Langenscheidt Publishing Group

BULGARIA

Kürdzhali

Veles

MACEDONIA

Durrës
Tiranë
Kičevo
Prilep

Sérres
Dhráma
Xánthi
Kavála

Elbasan
Bitola
Langadhás

Edessa
Thessaloníki
Thássos

ALBANIA
Florina
Véria
Halkidhikí
Thássos

Vlorë
Korçë
Kozáni
Kateríni
Athos

Sarandë
Grevená
Olympos 2917
Pineios
Sithonia
Límnos

Kérkyra (Corfu)
Ioánnina
Elassóna
Kassándra
Mýrina

Kérkyra (Corfu)
Igoumenítsa
Tríkala
Lárisa
AEGEAN

Paxí
Párga
Arta
Karditsa
Fársala
Vólos
Yioúra
Pipéri
Aghios Efstrátios
SEA

Andipaxi
GREECE
Alónissos
Skiáthos
Skýros
Sporades

Préveza
Lamía
Ag. Konstandínos
Skópelos

Lefkádha
Lefkádha (Léfkas)
Agrínio
Ámfissa
Evvia (Euboea)

Astakós
Ithiki
Náfpaktos
Chalkida
Paralía Kýmis

Argostóli
Livádhia
Kefalloniá
Pátra
Korinthiakos Kolpos
Athína (ATHENS)
Ándhros

Zákynthos
Pelo`nnisos (Peloponnese)
Korinthos
Piréas
Kéa

Zákynthos
Pýrgos
Árgar
Náfplio
Salamina
Éghina
Yiáros
Tínos

IONIAN
Trípoli
Póros
Kýthnos
Sýros
Cyclades
Páros

SEA
Spétses
Argo-Saronic Islands
Sérifos
Sífnos
Andíparos
Íos
Sikinos

Kalamáta
Spárti
Kímolos
Milos
Folégandhros

Gýthio
Neápoli

Kýthira

MEDITERRANEAN

Antikýthira

SEA

Kastélli Kissámou
Haniá (Chania)
Kríti (Crete)

Iráklion (Heraklíon)

Western Greece

Gavdhos

50 km / 30 miles

Welcome

This guidebook combines the interests and enthusiasms of two of the world's best-known information providers: Insight Guides, who have set the standard for visual travel guides since 1970, and Discovery Channel, the world's premier source of non-fiction television programming. Its aim is to help visitors get the most out of Corfu during a short stay of a week or two, and to this end Insight's main expert on Greece and its islands, Elizabeth Boleman-Herring, has created a series of carefully crafted itineraries. The tours link the island's highlights, but also explore many delightful corners that only someone intimately acquainted with Corfu is likely to know. They take in monasteries, churches, markets, offshore islets, secluded bays and even alternative health centres.

Supporting the itineraries are sections on history and culture, shopping, eating out and nightlife, plus a detailed practical information section, which includes a list of hand-picked hotels and pensions.

Elizabeth Boleman-Herring first went to Corfu, or Kérkyra, as the Greeks call it, in 1961. She says of that first visit, 'My mother was reading to me from a first edition of Gerald Durrell's hysterical account of his Corfiot childhood, and my family all swam endlessly in the incredible turquoise sea off the east coast, giggling over passages from *My Family and Other Animals*. Someone bought me my first bikini – blue and white polka dots – in Kérkyra Town, but I promptly lost the top half in the sea, and so became an early advocate of Hellenic toplessness. I remember crying bitterly when compelled to return to school in Athens.'

Boleman-Herring has often returned to that azure Ionian Sea, forging strong bonds on neighbouring Kefalloniá and Itháki. But her true favourites among the Ionians are Corfu, the tiny Dhiapóndia islets which are part and parcel of Kérkyra, and nearby Paxí – pristine, sophisticated – and also revisited in this guide.

Pages 2–3: the beach at Sidhári
Pages 8–9: icons on display at Angelókastro

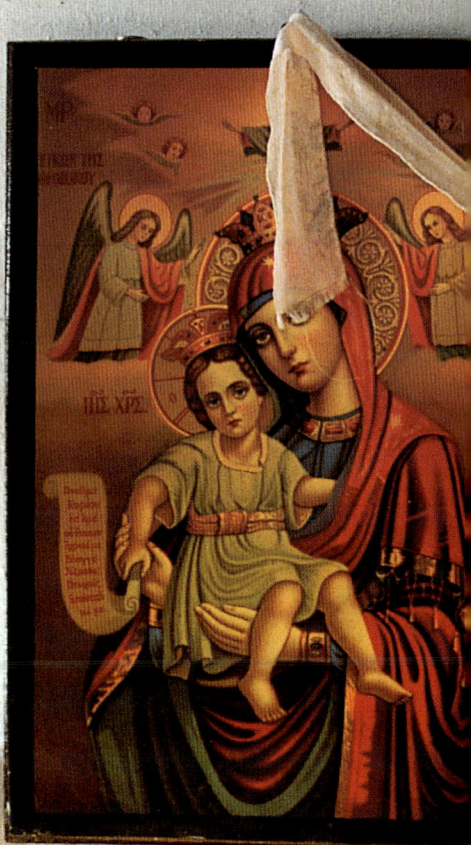

plunderers and builders, who carted off the ancient stones for use in their own bastions and mansions. It wasn't long before Corcyra rose up against its colonial master and sought independence. In 660BC, history's first ever recorded naval battle took place between Corcyra and Corinth, though history failed to record who won. Skirmishes between the two great naval powers continued, with the last great conflagration, waged near the islets of Sybota in 433BC, causing the great Peloponnesian War (431–404BC).

They Came, They Saw, They Conquered

Civil war on Corcyra followed, between the island's aristocrats (favouring Corinth and Sparta) and its democrats (siding with Athens). After much bloodshed, Corcyra fell to the Lacedaemonian general, Kleonymos, in 303BC; then, in 301BC, to Agathokles, Tyrant of Syracuse, and to Ptolemy in 284BC. A pattern was emerging in this corner of the Ionian Sea: the rich pearl that was Corfu – rich for strategic purposes as well as for its natural resources – would be snatched by successive waves of invaders. Corfiot history, from the 3rd century BC on, may be seen as a revolving door of European predation, though those who came to plunder invariably left something of value in their wake.

Distinguishing between pirates and protectors must have proved difficult for the Corfiots, since a veritable parade of both were subsequently to descend upon the island. A glance at a map hints at the reason, and shows a remarkable geographic similarity to the 'great boot' of Italy – Corfu resembles a little boot, its ankle symbolically flexed back to kick something away. The ancients saw the island as a harp or scythe shape, and named it accordingly, but the modern name comes from the Greek word *korýfo*, after the pair of summits now crowned by the Old and New Fortresses.

The Romans, provoked beyond endurance by attacks on their mariners by Illyrian pirates, declared war on them in around 229BC. The Illyrians,

Above: the great Peloponnesian War

in turn, laid siege to Corfu, but the island was immediately liberated by Caius Fulvius, and placed itself willingly under the protection of its powerful neighbour. The Romans would stay on for the next five centuries, and some illustrious Italians visited Corcyra: Cicero and Cato; Marc Antony and Octavia; Agrippina and her children, Julia and Caligula.

In AD40 two disciples of St Paul, saints Jason and Sosipater, brought Christianity to Corfu and established the island's first church, St Stephen's – which explains the plethora of modern place names reading Agios or San (Saint) Stefanos around the island.

Following the splitting of the Roman Empire by Diocletian late in the 3rd century into western and eastern portions – the latter to become Byzantium – Corfu's regime changed. It was to remain, on and off, a possession of Byzantium until 1204, which saw the fall of Constantinople. This great capital was the cradle of Orthodoxy, and the fall of 'The City' is still considered by Greeks to be, after the Crucifixion, the darkest day in history. Life between the 4th and 13th centuries was – here as in most of Europe – nasty, short and brutish, with a series of invaders storming the twin peaks. The Vandals sacked the island in 455, followed by the Goths in 550; the Saracens attacked repeatedly between the 7th and 11th centuries. In 1081 the island was taken by the Normans, under Robert Guiscard; they were subsequently defeated by the Venetians, but then returned under Bohemond, Robert's son, only to be defeated by the Byzantines... to return again under Robert's nephew, Roger II of Sicily! No wonder the islanders finally took to the heights of the town and erected strong walls.

For three weeks during 1203, the bays were filled with the vast fleet of the Fourth Crusade, which weighed anchor here on its way to sack Constantinople. It was an awesome display, but for once the fleet had their sights on a richer trophy than the little Ionian isle.

The Most Serene Republic

Much of what we regard today as 'Corfiot' – the Old and New Fortresses, the narrow streets *(kantoúnia)* and their elegant residences, the lovely cobbled squares and Italianate churches, the Roman Catholic cathedral, the elaborately decorated government buildings – is, in fact, Venetian.

Of all the conquerors and administrators, pirates and protectors that Corfu has seen, none left such an impression as The Most Serene Republic. The Venetians, who occupied Corfu for a mere 400 years (compared with the millennium of Byzantine and Frankish domination), left a distinctive mark on the island's skyline, its social organisation, its forms of cultural impression – even its cuisine – that remains to this day. One may still sit on the Spianádha, a lovely town green originally cleared to give a free field for Venetian artillery, dining on Venetian delicacies in the company of a direct descendant of someone listed among the 'first families' in the Venetian *Libro d'Oro* and

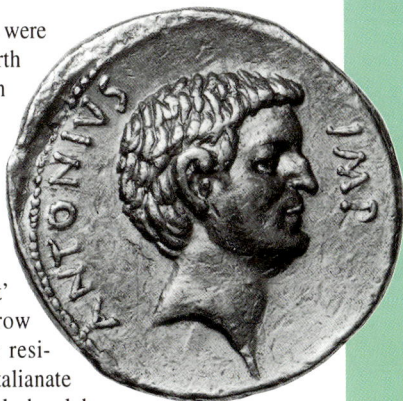

Right: the head of Marc Antony, a Roman visitor to Corfu

be serenaded by musicians singing Venetian *Kandádhes*. It is as though the Serenis-
sima (the 'Most Serene' republic) has only
recently – and temporarily – departed.

Venetians came to Corfu to govern and
plant olive trees, not simply to plunder,
and they built fortresses to repel the most
determined of foes. There were, of course,
Byzantine and Angevin forts on Corfu
before the Venetians, but these were built
to safeguard garrisons, rather than to protect the people. Venice strove to fortify all
of Corfu, assigning its military architects
to the construction of the defences, with
a network of tunnels to maintain commu-
nications in time of siege.

The Venetians were invitees, not conquerors – their assistance had been sought
to ward off the attentions of the ruler of
Padua in 1386. In 1387 a treaty that was to
hold for the next 410 years formalised rela-
tions between the Doge and Corfu's nobil-
ity. Venice was to defend Corfu, but was
barred from intervening in its feudal affairs,
where the rich remained aloof and powerful, the poor went hungry and served
the rich, and a middle class did not exist at all until after the 17th century.

In addition to all the civic building, the Venetians also brought organised
Roman Catholicism to Corfu, ushering in a period of religious tension
that was compounded by their motto, 'We are first Venetians, and then
Christians'. Many Corfiots felt themselves to be first Greek Orthodox,
second Christians, and Corfiots subservient to Venice as a distant third.

Barbarians at the Gate

All, however, were united in supporting the motto: 'First: NOT DEAD at
the hands of the Genoese or, heaven forbid, the Ottoman Turks.' Any threat
to Venetian peace over the next four centuries came primarily from without, not within. The Genoese spearheaded the agression, first in 1403 with
their failed attempt to storm Angelókastro – visitors to this remarkable
castle on the west coast will wonder why any besieger would even try.

The Ottoman Turks were a more formidable foe than Genoa, laying siege
to the island five times between 1430 and 1716, but still Corfu was spared
the fate of most of the rest of Greece and never fell beneath the Turkish
yoke – due entirely to the fortifications erected by Venice. The final siege,
mounted early in the 18th century, was repulsed due to the heroic efforts
of Saxon Field-Marshal Johann Matthias von der Schulenburg, aided by
the timely arrival of Maltese Knights of St John, along with reinforcements
from Spain, Genoa and Venice itself. The siege and the battles waged during the first half of 1716 are the stuff of legends, and the victory was credited

Above: Coptic angel, a sign of eastern influence

to the other-worldly intervention of the island's patron saint, Spyrídhon, whereupon it was decreed that there would be an annual procession on 11 August to honour the saint. On a more terrestrial level, a statue of Schulenburg, now outside the entrance to the Old Fortress, was commissioned, and Vivaldi composed a commemorative oratorio.

French and British Intervention

Delivered from the east, and, as it were, the past, Corfu now entered the modern age, and yet foreign occupiers were still to arrive, in the form of the revolutionary French. They came in peace in 1797 and stayed on to liberate the serfs, establish free trade and shock the locals with their atheism.

Defeated by a Russo-Turkish fleet in 1799, the French departed, and in 1800 the Ionian islands finally achieved a sort of independent nationhood as the Septinsular State. John Kapodhistrias, as first Minister of the Interior, reformed the island's fiscal system and, in so doing, dealt a death blow to the long-entrenched Corfiot aristocracy. Between 1804 and 1807, Corfu, for the first time in its long history, began to attract some prosperity.

But it was not to last. In August 1807, the imperial French annexed the Ionians and held them until April 1814, when, following Napoleon's defeat, the British peacefully occupied Corfu. A year later they were ceded all of the Ionians. The first British High Commissioner, Thomas Maitland, was instrumental in establishing a constitution, Greek Orthodoxy was declared the state religion and Greek the official language – something of a problem for Kérkyra's large, Italian-speaking, Jewish and aristocratic communities.

The British left a lasting legacy – monuments, fortifications, public works. Although the Ionian Greeks' desire for union with Greece became vociferous, the transition, when it came, was peaceful. Given leave to select the successor to the deposed German King Otto of the Greeks, the British chose Crown Prince George Glücksburg of Denmark. As a condition of acceding the Greek throne, George I (as he would become) demanded that Britain cede the Ionian islands to his kingdom, and so on 16 May 1864, the act of termination of the 'British protection' was signed.

Today, though cricket is still played by Corfiots, Corfu is quintessentially Greek. It is now part of a regional governmental unit that votes Socialist and depends on tourism.

But more conservative culturally, Corfiots cling to their Christian faith and traditional Greek mores: the family is all, and hard work, to provide for the next generation's education and improvement, is axiomatic. Tending the millions of olive trees that comprise one of Venice's greatest living legacies to Corfu, Greece and Europe, and serving the new invaders of summer are the islanders' two primary objectives. But everyone on Corfu can always make time for 'philharmonic society' (read marching brass band) practice, and for honouring St Spyrídhon.

Right: Corfu became part of Napoleon's empire

St Spyrídhon, the Spirit of Corfu

Speaking of Corfu and its patron saint, Lawrence Durrell wrote: 'The island is really the Saint: and the Saint is the island.' For in Greece, each place has its own reverend patron and so does each individual Greek – a saint whose name he bears and whose annual name day he celebrates. In the case of a huge number of male Corfiots, this is St Spyrídhon.

The saint is Corfu's most revered and influential resident, his mummy encased in a silver reliquary and enthroned like royalty in the red-domed church that bears his name. The faithful who bend to kiss his tiny slippers would never countenance the fact that Spyrídhon was not always a saint, nor ever, indeed, a Corfiot. Born in the middle of the 4th century AD, he became a shepherd in the mountains of Cyprus, but though poor and uneducated he attained a reputation for piety, self-sacrifice and wisdom. He married, but his beloved wife died giving birth to his only child, Irini. When she came of age she was made a nun, and her father retired into a monastery.

Eventually, he was named Bishop of Trimithion, and accounts of his Solomon-like wisdom began to be recorded, mixing legend and fact. There are stories of miracles performed during his lifetime, but none compares with those the saint accomplished after his death in AD350. In life, Spyrídhon may have confined himself to meting out individual justice and homely logic; in death he would rout Turk, plague and famine.

Spyrídhon's body was taken to Constantinople during the 7th century but by the mid-15th century that city was no longer safe for Christians, alive or dead, and George Kaloheiritis, the priest in whose church St Spyrídhon reposed, decided to move his holy charge. He set out across what is now northern Greece and eventually came to Corfu, where he married and produced three sons, to whom he willed the holy relics. His son, Phillip, also a priest, considered moving Spyrídhon to Venice, but the Corfiots' tearful entreaties stopped him.

The Church of the Miracleworking St Spyrídhon in Kérkyra is filled with votive offerings. There are four great miracles performed by the saint on behalf of his island that are commemorated by processing his relics through the town. The first is commemorated on Easter Saturday, celebrating St Spyrídhon's deliverance of the island from famine; the Palm Sunday procession recalls Corfu's salvation from plague in 1629; the first Sunday in November marks its deliverance from cholera in 1673. The last great miracle was performed on 24 June 1716, when St Spyrídhon is said to have appeared to the Ottoman army, holding a 'sword flashing lightning and furiously pursuing them'. The Ottomans fled, and the fourth annual procession of the saint was instituted on 11 August.

For the people of Corfu, the saint is both a touchstone and a talisman. The finest greeting and farewell in Corfu is: 'O Ághios Spyrídhomas mazí sou' – 'May St Spyrídhon be with you'.

Left: candles to St Spyrídhon

HISTORY HIGHLIGHTS

70,000–40,000BC Prehistoric inhabitation of the island.

750BC Eretrians, Greeks from Euboea, subdue Illyrian Liburnians, Corfu's first documented residents.

734BC Led by Chersicrates, Corinthians colonise Corcyra, at Kanóni.

660BC First naval battle in history fought between Corinth and Corcyra.

433BC Battle between Corinth and Corcyra leads to Peloponnesian War.

427–425BC Corcyran civil war between aristocrats and democrats.

229BC Illyrians mount siege of Corcyra; Romans seize power.

AD37–41 Jason, Bishop of Tarsus, and Sosipater, the Bishop of Ikonium, disciples of St Paul, bring Christianity to Corcyra.

325 Spyrídhon, Bishop of Trimithion, Cyprus, participates in First Ecumenical Synod of Nicaea. He is later canonised.

Late 3rd century AD Emperor Diocletian divides Roman Empire into western and eastern halves; Corcyra becomes part of the Eastern Roman, later Byzantine Empire.

455 Vandals sack Corcyra.

550 Goths sack Corcyra.

1081 Normans, under Robert Guiscard, seize island; subsequent Imperial Byzantine and Venetian incursions.

1191 Final expulsion of Normans by Byzantines.

1203 Fourth Crusade stops off at Corfu en route to Constantinople.

1204 Constantinople falls to Latin Catholics.

1205 Venetians seize Corfu, dividing it, in 1207, among 10 feudal lords of Venice.

1267 According to the Treaty of Viterbo, the Angevins, of Naples, are ceded Corfu, and exploit its vineyards, olives and salt pans.

1267–1386 During Angevin rule, Corfu's Jewish community burgeons.

1386 Venice, invited by the Corfiots, takes possession of the island on 28 May. Venetian domination extends until 1797, sparing Corfu the ravages of Ottoman Turkish rule.

1493 New wave of Jews arrive, fleeing the Inquisition in Spain.

1537 First great Turkish siege of Corfu; countryside sacked and islanders carried off as slaves.

1576–88 Venice erects great city walls and fortresses at Kérkyra.

1571 Second Ottoman siege.

1716 Great Ottoman siege repulsed by Corfiots, Venetians and allies, under Saxon Field-Marshal Johann Matthias von der Schulenburg; victory attributed to St Spyrídhon's intervention.

1722–8 Kérkyra is further fortified.

1797–9 Following Napoleon's defeat of Venice, Ionian islands are ceded to the French Republic.

1799 Russians and Turks defeat French and seize island.

1800–7 The semi-independent Septinsular state established by Russia and Turkey, under President Count Spyrídhon-George Theotokis.

1807–14 Russians cede Ionians to the Imperial French.

1815 With the Treaty of Paris, the Ionians fall under British Protection.

1823 Ionian Academy, first modern Greek university, founded.

1823 John Kapodhistrias elected first president of Independent Greece.

1864 King George of Greece arrives on 21 May; Protectorate ends.

1941 Corfu surrenders to Italy.

1943 Nazis occupy the island, execute Italian officers, and remove Jews to Germany for extermination.

1944 Germans depart after blowing up harbour installations.

1951 Club Mediterranée opens in Ýpsos.

1994 Corfu is the site of the European summit meeting.

2002 Greece adopts the euro.

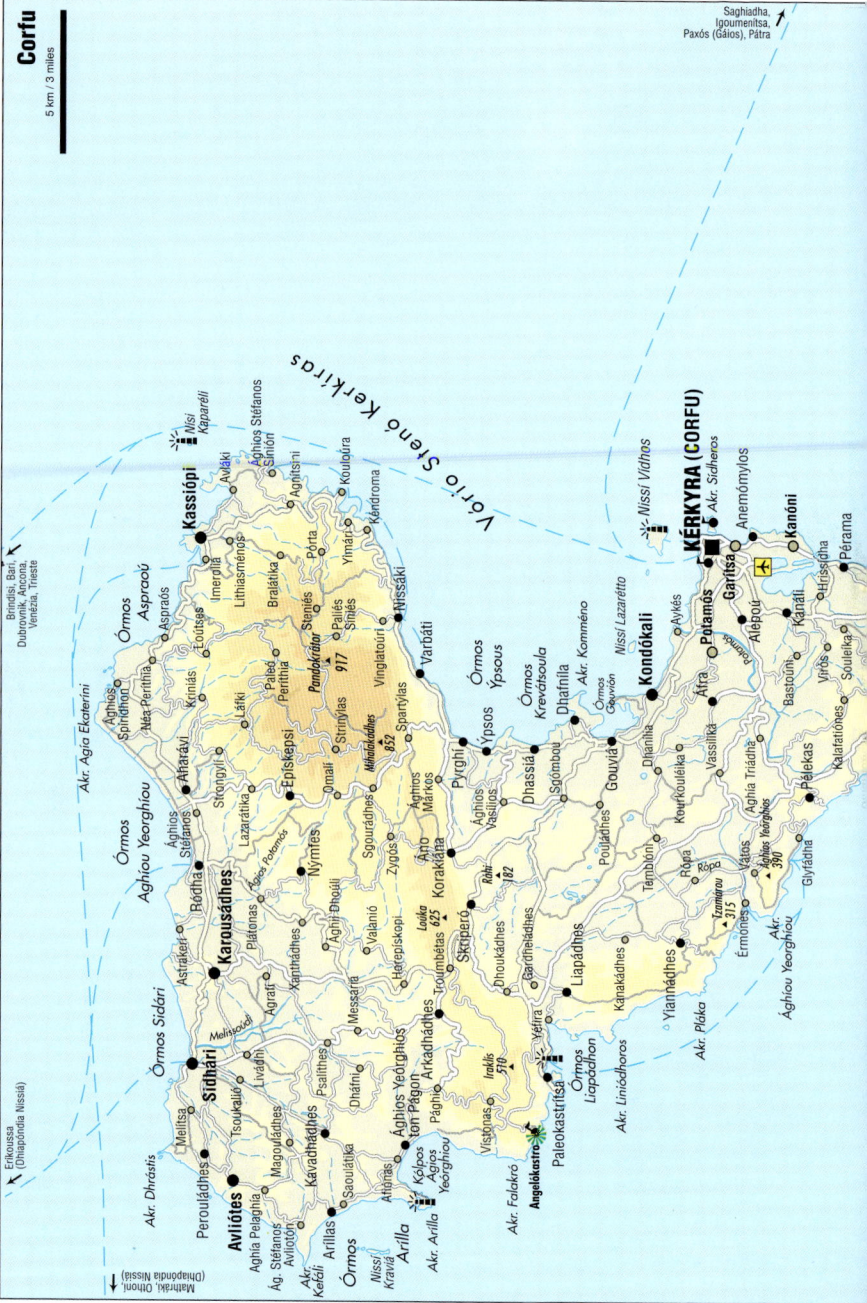

Corfu

5 km / 3 miles

Saghiadha,
Igoumenitsa,
Paxós (Gáios), Pátra

Brindisi, Bari,
Dubrovnik, Ancona,
Venezia, Trieste

Vório Stenó Kerkíras

Eríkoussa
(Othiapóndia Nissiá)

Akr. Agia Ekaterini

Akr. Dhrástis

Órmos Sidhári

Melitsód

Sidhári
Perouládhes
Aghia Pelaghia
Avliótes
Ag. Stéfanos
Avliotón
Kavadhádhes
Magouládhes
Livádi
Tsoukaló
Psalíthes
Dhafní
Saoulátika
Afiónas
Akr. Kefáli
Arillas
Órmos
Nissí
Kraviá
Akr. Arilla
Arilla

Matraki, Othoni,
(Othonía Nissiá)

Karousádhes
Astrakerí
Platónas
Aghií Dhoúli
Xanthádhes
Agrafí
Messariá
Agros Potamós
Ráchi
Valanió
Héripiskopi
Loúka
625
Skriperó
Giannádhes
Kanakádhes

Akr. Agia Ekaterini
Órmos Aghiou Yeorghiou
Ródha
Aghios Stéfanos
Lazarátika
Strongylí
Nymfes
Sgourádhes
Zygós
Áno Korakiána
Rohi
162
Dhoukádhes
Gardhelades
Liapádhes

Aghios Spiridhon
Áno Perithia
Krinías
Loútses
Paleó Perithia
Láfki
Épiskepsi
Omalí
Stranylas
Nistoládhes
852
Pyrghi
Aghios
Márkos
Aghios
Vasílios
Dhassiá
Sgómbou
Gouviá
Pouládhes
Tembloni
Ágios
Yeorghios
ton Págon
Pághio Arkadhádhes
Troumbétas
Yéfira
Vistónas
Iraklis
510
Akr. Falakró
Angelókastro
Paleokastrítsa

Avláki
Aghios Stéfanos
Sinióti
Aghitsíni
Kassiópi
Pórta
Yimári
Kéndroma
Nissáki
Akr. Kommèno
Órmos Ypsous
Órmos Krevátsoula
Dhafnila
Órmos Gèovón
Kondókali
Imerólía
Lithiasménos
Braiátika
Pandokrátor
917
Vinglatoúri
Varbáti
Strinýlas
Spartylas
Ypsos
Kouloúra
Órmos
Liapádhon
Akr. Plóka
Akr. Liniódhoros

Nissí
Kaparéli

KÉRKYRA (CORFU)
Akr. Sidheros
Anemómylos
Garitsá
Potamós
Alepoú
Kanóni
Kanáli
Hrisídha
Pérama
Afra
Vátos
Kouvouléika
Ágios Yeorghios
Glyfádha
Akr. Aghiou Yeorghiou
Vassiliká
Aghía Triádha
Bastoúni
Vírós
Soulèka
Akr.
Órmos
Ròpa
Ròpa
Tzavrou
915
Ermónes
390
Pelekas
Kalafationes
Pelekas
Nissi Vidhas
Nissí Vidhos
Nissí Lazarétto
Aklés
Dhiniha

Akr. Kefáli

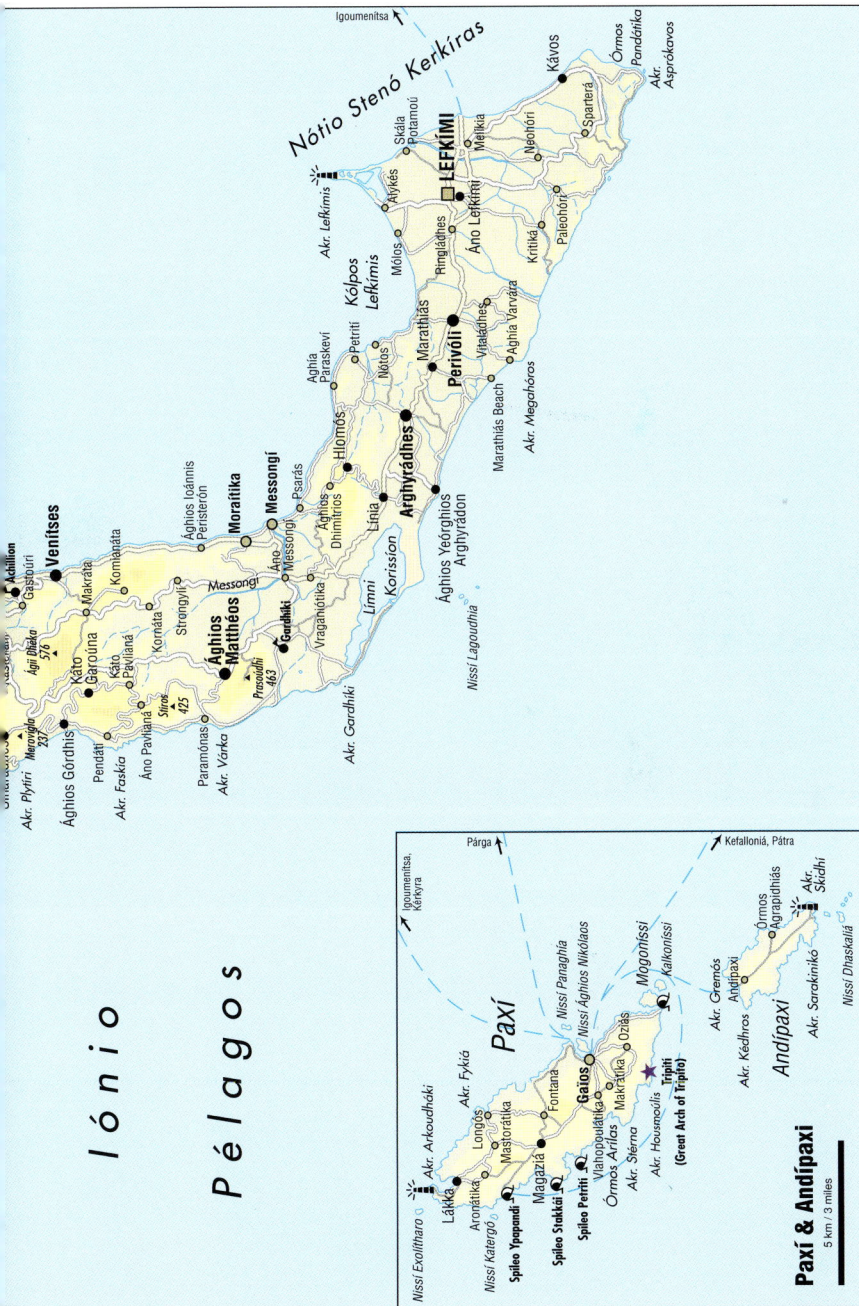

Igoumenítsa

Nótio Stenó Kerkíras

Skála Potamoú
□ **LEFKÍMI**

Kávos
Órmos
Pandókva
Akr.
Asprókavos

Sparterá

Akr. Lefkímis

Alýkes

Melíkia

Neohóri

Áno Lefkími

Paleohóri

Rímgládhes

*Kólpos
Lefkímis*

Kritiká

Mólos

Akr. Lefkímis

Nótos

Marathiás

Perivóli

Vitaládhes

Aghía Varvára

Aghía
Paraskeví

Petríti

Marathiás Beach

Akr. Megahóros

Hlomós

Arghyrádhes

Aghía
Dhimítrios

Linia

Psárás

Ághios Ioánnis
Peristerón

Moraítika

Áno
Messóngi

Messóngi

Ághios Veórghios
Arghyrádon

Nissí Lagoudhía

Ághios Ioánnis
Peristerón

Líria

*Limní
Korissíon*

Vraganótika

Strongylí

Achíllion
Venítses

Gastoúri

Makráta

Komianáta

Messóngi

Kornáta

**Ághios
Matthéos**
463

Gardhíki

Áno Pavliána

*Siros
425*

Prasoúdhi
463

Akr. Gardhíki

Akr. Plytíri
Merovígli
233

Agii Dhéka
576

Ághios Górdhis

Pendáti

Káto
Garoúna

Káto
Pavliána

Paramónas

Akr. Várka

Akr. Faskía

Iónio

Pélagos

Párga

Kefalloniá, Pátra

*Igoumenítsa,
Kérkyra*

Órmos
Agrapidhiás

Akr.
Skídhi

Nissí Panaghía

Paxí

Mogoníssi

Kalkoníssi

Akr. Gremós

Andípaxi

Andípaxi

Akr. Kédhros

Akr. Sarakinikó

Nissí Dhaskaliá

Nissí Ághios Nikolaos

Ozíás

Akr. Arkoudháki

Akr. Fykió

Nissí Exolítharo

Lákka

Longós

Aroníátika

Nissí Katergó

Spíleo Ypapandí

Mastorátika

Magaziá

Fontána

Vlahopúlátika

Gaíos

Makrátika

Tripití
(**Great Arch of Tripití**)

Órmos Arílas

Akr. Sférna

Akr. Housmoúlis

Spíleo Petríti

Spíleo Staktaí

Paxí & Andípaxi

5 km / 3 miles

Órmos Ághíou Nikoláou

(St Nicholas Bay)

Mandraki Harbour

Itinerary 1
Itinerary 2
Itinerary 5
Itinerary 14

Aghios Yeorghios

Old Fortress Café

Palió Enetikó Froúrio (Old Venetian Fortress)

Contrafossa

Faliraki Complex
ALÉKOU
Reading Society & Rotary Club
Museum of Asian Art
Palace of St Michael & St George
Municipal Gallery
Art Café & Bar
Panaghía Mandhrakioú
Statue of Guilford
Statue of Schulenburg
Enossi Monument
Maitland's Rotunda
Statue of Kapodhistrias

Statue of Adam
Cricket Ground
SPIANÁDHA (ESPLANADE)
Bandstand
Statue of Kapodhistrias

Panaghía Andívouniótissa
Byzantine Museum

Viktóros Dhousmán

Kapodhistríou

CAMPIELLO

Well of Kremasti
Panaghía Spyridhon
Ton Xénon
Aghios Ioánnis
La Famiglia
La Favorita
Mitrópoli-Corfu Cathedral
Catholic Cathedral
Ionian Academy

Summer Cinema Phoenix

Nissí Vidhos

Old Port

Arsenálou
Panaghía Andívouniótissa

Aghii Patéres
Komnonário

Aghios Andréas
Town Hall
Jazz Rock Garden
Ionian Parliament
Holy Trinity Anglican Church

Archaeological Museum

Dhimokratías

Velissaríou
Scuola Greca

Municipal Theatre

Dresslla
Prefecture
OTE
Police H.Q.

Rizospáston Voulefón

Polyla

Vralia

SAN ROCCO

Alexándhras

Marasli

Patriárhou Athínagóra
ELPA-Automobile & Touring Club of Greece

Venetian Gates
Platía Solomoú
Panaghía Tenédhou
Platía Néou Froufríou

Xenofóndos Stratigoú

Neo Enetikó Froúrio (New Venetian Fortress)

Ioánnou Theotóki
Platía San Rocco
Medi Jeunesse

Mitropóliti-Methodhíou

ANGLIKÓ NEKROTAFÍO (BRITISH CEMETERY)

Kelokotróni

Avramíou
Ionian University

Polyhroníou Konstandá

Platía Psyhiatríou

Dhimoulitsa

Menhí Hospital

Kandakalí

Alepoú

Alepoú

Corfu (Kérkyra) Town

200 m / 220 yards

Órmos Garítsas

(Garitsa Bay)

Dhimokratías

Douglas Obelisk

Menekrátous

Menekrates Monument

M. Athanassiou

Marasli

Dimfrou

Kyprou

Sofianou

Kavoura

GARITSA

Aghios Triádha

Othnissós

Dhessila

Krus Smyrnis

Vlahernón

Ethnikoú Stádhion

Yeorgáki

Lefkímis

Lefkimi

Anapávseos

Dhessila

Dörpfeld

Dörpfeld

ORTHODOX CEMETERY

Airport

Prison

A. Dhari

A. Dhari

Dhimokratías

Aghii Iáson keh Sosípatros

Nafsikas

ANEMÓMYLOS

Tásonos Sosipátrou

E. Theotóki

Emmanouil Theotóki

Aghia Evfimía

Paleópolis

Temple of Juno

Temple of Diana

PALEÓPOLIS

MON REPOS BEACH

Mon Repos Harbour

Corfu *Itineraries*

1. THE HISTORIC CENTRE *(see map, p20–1)*

This walking tour takes in the Archaeological Museum of Corfu Town (Kérkyra), the Old Fortress, the Museum of Asian Art (housed in the Palace of St Michael and St George) and the Church of the Miracle-Working St Spyrídhon. Lunch on Kapodhistríou Street, an afternoon swim at Mon Repos and dinner at La Famiglia round out this full day of activities. Be sure to call and reserve a table at La Famiglia (tel: 26610 30270).

To the starting point: the corniche of Garítsa Bay, Dhimokratías Avenue, is easily accessible from all Kérkyra hotels. Follow it until, midway around the bay, between the Old Fortress to the north and the Mon Repos beach 'club' to the south, you reach Vraïla Street.

For this day's walking tour of the historic centre it is wise to first breakfast well at your hotel, then set out in comfortable shoes – any day but Monday – armed with sunhat and sunblock if you are there in summer, to arrive at the Archaeological Museum of Corfu as early as possible.

The **Archaeological Museum of Corfu** (tel: 26610 30680; daily 8.30am–3pm, closed Mon; entrance fee) is situated half a block up Vraïla Street from its junction with Dhimokratías Avenue. On the ground floor are some nicely detailed small bronze statuettes dating from the Archaic, Roman and Hellenistic periods. Here too is the stunning silver ceremonial helmet of a Hellenistic general (complete with gold myrtle-berry and acorn chaplet), together with his iron armour, swords, battle helmet, oil-scrapers (for personal hygiene), protective shoulder epaulets and bronze burial urn, all dating from the 4th century BC.

Early Cycladic (3rd millennium BC) violin-shaped marble statuettes and a marble, crater-shaped *kandhíla* (oil lamp) – recovered from thieves of Greek antiquities – complete the ground-floor displays. Plexiglas maps on the first-floor landing detail Corfu's ancient cities and archaeological sites, human habitations dating from 40,000BC up to and including the Roman period. You might want to pick up a copy of the concise history and guide, *Ancient Kérkyra*, by Alkestis Spetsieri-Choremi (available in English and German at the ticket desk), which details the island's early history and significant finds.

Proceed into the central upstairs hall, to be confronted by the prone Archaic carved Lion of the Menekrates, from the 7th century BC. The galleries to the east, accessed by a separate door from the stairway, contain a dozen or so clay figurines of the

Left: the Church of St George
Right: Corinthian lion

goddess Artemis in her avatar as the Mistress of Animals, cradling beasts ranging from deer to lion cubs. These are representative of the 6,000-plus idols found in the 480BC Temple of Artemis on the Mon Repos estate near Kanóni. In the same room is a fragment of an Archaic pediment from the 5th century BC, which depicts a Dionysian symposium – the god Dionysos, wielding a drinking horn, and a youth recline on a couch, beneath which a lion is being cornered by a hunting hound. A small limestone head of a *kouros*, dating from 535–530BC, and an early example of statuary bearing the enigmatic 'Archaic Smile', was executed by a Corinthian sculptor.

In the aqua-walled **Gorgon Room** looms the monumental Gorgon (or Medusa) Pediment, dated 590–580BC, a fragment of the Doric Temple of Artemis. A strangely Asiatic figure, Medusa, the mother of Chrysaor (the diminutive figure to the right) and the winged horse, Pegasus (formerly on her left, now missing), is frightful even by 21st-century standards, with her protuberant eyes and serpentine locks. (In myth, the hero Perseus cut off her head without looking at her directly, lest he be turned to stone, and her two offspring were born, simultaneously, of her spilt blood.)

Leave the museum now and go back to Dhimokratías Avenue, turning left towards the Old Fortress, your next destination. Follow the corniche along the bay, passing the luxurious Corfu Palace Hotel on your left. The Old Fortress will be clearly visible for the duration of your 5- to 10-minute walk, with a backdrop of the denuded mountains of Albania.

Proceed gently uphill on the seaward side of Dhimokratías Avenue. You will be overtaken by brightly painted horse-drawn carriages, available for hire on

Above: the Gorgon Pediment
Left: Maitland Rotunda

itineraries

the grand central esplanade, or 'Spianádha' ahead. Pass, on your left, a marble statue of the illustrious Corfiot, Count John Kapodhistrias, first president of the independent Greek state. Bear right along Dhimokratías Avenue, with the Spianádha on your left and the Café Aktaion on your right.

The Venetian Legacy

The **Spianádha**, Kérkyra's grand central park, serves as a meeting place for the entire capital in summer. Established by the Venetians for strategic purposes, and maintained by subsequent occupying forces, the Spianádha is now used for rest and recreation and, at the far northern end, for cricket matches in the spring and summer. Look to your left as you walk, and you will see within the park reminders of the British occupation: the Rotunda (known to the locals as the 'Stérna', as it was once the site of the town's cistern), erected in memory of the first British High Commissioner, Sir Thomas Maitland; and the Bandstand (or 'Pálko'), where open-air concerts are staged by the many Corfiot philharmonic societies – massive brass bands – throughout the summer.

Directly opposite the hire centre for horse-drawn carriages is the entrance to the **Paleó Froúrio** (Old Fortress; tel: 26610 48311; daily 9am–7pm; entrance fee). Proceed directly across the iron bridge which spans the Venetian-dug moat (the *Contrafossa*), today lined with Corfiot boat sheds and dotted with local fishing boats. To left and right, you can see massive twin bastions that were constructed by the Venetians during the 16th century. Over the Main Gate, a 19th-century inscription commissioned by King George I of the Greeks reads, 'My strength is the love of the people'.

On your left, before entering the enceinte proper, you will find an excellent **Ministry of Culture Museum Shop** (tel: 26610 46919; Mon–Fri 8.30am–3pm), a good source of information and fine souvenirs. There are casts of sculptures from many Greek museums, copies of icons from Corfu's Byzantine Museum, books, cards and reproduction jewellery. Mr Spyros Margaritis, who works here, is very knowledgeable, not only about the fortress, but also about Corfu's history in general.

On your right, do not miss the permanent exhibition entitled **Byzantine Collection of Corfu** (Mon–Fri 8.30am–3pm), also housed in the gatehouse and comprising early Christian finds from Paleopolis (near present-day Kanóni) and Káto Korakiána (in central Corfu, near Dhassiá). There are floor mosaics on display, as well as marble architectural fragments from the early basilica, and beautiful ecclesiastical wall paintings.

Entering the fortress proper you will see, to left and right, the land moat,

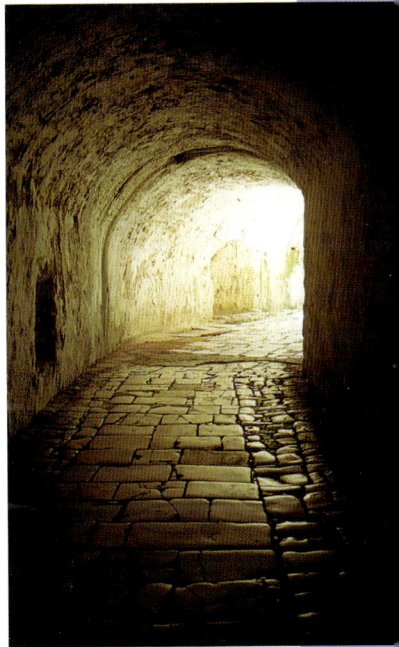

Right: gallery through the Old Fortress

and pass the Roman Catholic Chapel of the Madonna Dei Carmini (now used as a workshop for icon restoration). Pass beneath Corfu's Archives and Public Library, formerly the British Barracks. Proceed right, following signs for St George's Church and the **Old Fortress Café** (tel: 26610 48550; daily 9am– 2am). A flight of stairs on your left takes you up by stages to the Land Tower. The café, with its splendid view of Garítsa Bay, is to your right as you ascend. It is a nice, cool place to return to for a meal or a drink – and becomes a popular late-night venue after dark.

With the Clock Tower on your left, proceed steeply uphill, passing through a fortified archway and cobbled tunnel, to view the coastline of Albania and Greek Epirus, and tiny Vídhos islet, site of the Serbian Cemetery, where some 40,000–50,000 casualties from World War I lie buried. Lazarétto islet, site of German executions of members of the Corfiot Resistance, is slightly further west.

Climb further on your right, passing the Venetian Prison. The ascent to the lighthouse is steep, but the view from the summit is worth the effort. Carefully retrace your steps to the Old Fortress Café, then proceed gently downhill to your right where you can see the imposing, spare, Parthenon-like facade of the **Church of St George of the Old Fortress** (Ághios Yeórghios tou Paleoú Frouríou). Incongruous here among the ramparts, this originally Anglican church was built during the years of the British Protectorate (1815–64), to a Doric/Georgian design (the interior was sadly altered by the Nazi bombardment of Corfu in September 1943). Converted to a Greek Orthodox sanctuary in 1865, the beautiful, simple interior affords a peaceful respite after your hike round the battlements.

Gardens and Galleries

Now head across the vast, gravelled parade grounds, with the café uphill to your right. To the right, you'll find the way out of the Old Fortress, passing a fussy, Carraran marble statue of Field-Marshal Count Johann Matthias von der Schulenburg, the Saxon soldier of fortune who saved the day – and Corfu – when the Ottoman Turks attacked in 1716. Proceed, anti-clockwise, around the Spianádha for about 23m (75ft), where you will pass a small park with a statue of the eccentric expatriate, the 5th Earl of Guilford (1769–1828), who gave Greece its first modern university. Just beyond Guilford Park is the small terracotta-and-burgundy **Church of Panaghía Mandhrakíou**. An iron gate adjacent to the church leads into yet another garden and the Municipal Gallery's Art Café and Bar (tel: 26610 49366; daily 9.30am–midnight), which offers light snacks and beverages.

Leave the garden – you'll return to the gallery later on in your stay – and continue your ambulatory circuit of the Spianádha, now rounding the municipal cricket pitch on your left. The Municipal Art Gallery and the Museum of Asian Art are both housed in the imposing neoclassical Palace of St Michael and St George, built between 1819 and 1824 by Maltese stonemasons in honour of British citizens who served with distinction on Malta and throughout the Ionian islands. Before it, in a small park, stands a statue of British Lord High Commissioner, Sir Frederick Adam, who built an aqueduct for Kérkyra in 1832. (On summer evenings the pond at Adam's feet fills with large, noisy frogs, who sound like Aristophanes' ancient croakers.)

The **Museum of Asian Art** (tel: 26610 30443; daily 8.30am–3pm, closed Mon; entrance fee), which has been open to the public since 1923, is a distinct surprise, containing as it does fine holdings of Chinese, Japanese and Central, South and Southeast Asian art. Donated by four 20th-century Greek diplomat-collectors over a period of about 40 years, the collection is well documented in *Kerkyra: Museum of Asian Art*, by archaeologist Aglaia Karamanou-Papoutsani, which is readily available in Kérkyra.

On leaving the palace turn right, then sharp left down towards the Spianádha, watching out for oncoming traffic. The lovely colonnaded **Listón** (signed Leofóros Vasiléos Yeorghíou A) lies directly ahead – a marble-tiled pedestrian mall lined with upmarket cafés. Conceived by a Frenchman, Matthieu de Lesseps, the colonnade was built in 1807 and resembles the rue de Rivoli, with its oversized iron lanterns and covered arcade, or 'Volta'.

One street behind and parallel to the Listón is Kapodhistríou Street, and at Nos 23 and 66 respectively are two fine restaurants, the Aegli *(see page 73)* and the Rex *(see page 75)*, either of which is a fine place to stop for lunch (or return for dinner). Have a discreet peek in the kitchen before you order – you're sure to see something authentically Corfiot and delicious.

Above Left: Church of Panaghía Mandhrakíou. **Left:** icons of St Spyrídhon. **Right:** statue of Sir Frederick Adam

St Spyrídhon's Shrine

After lunch, retrace your route along Kapodhistríou Street and turn down intersecting Aghíou Spyrídhonos Street. Halfway down the block, you will see, rising on your left, the crimson-topped campanile of the 1590 founded **Church of the Miracleworking St Spyrídhon**, patron saint of Corfu *(see page 16)*. Quickly passing the ghastly souvenir shops, then the 18th-century Church of St Eleftherios and St Anna on your left, walk another 15m (50ft) or so till you

see the unassuming entrance to St Spyrídhon's. The entrance may be humble, but this structure is home to Corfu's holy of holies. Proceed, with due reverence, into the tiny room to the right of the iconostasis. Here you will be able to see the Viennese silver reliquary containing the mummified remains of the saint – which attracts Orthodox pilgrims from all over the world. As local tradition has it, the saint's slippers must be replaced periodically, when they are worn out from his supernatural visits among his flock.

Retracing your steps to the Spianádha, you have a 20- to 30-minute walk south to Mon Repos beach. Head south from the Spianádha on Dhimokratías Avenue, passing the Corfu Palace Hotel and Vraïla Street, making a complete circuit of Garítsa Bay, either along the seafront or in the shade of the avenue-long park. As you near the end of the bay, you pass the **Nautilus Café** (tel: 26610 49707; daily 8am–1am), where you can pause for a *frappé* (iced coffee) or a *tsitsibýra* (ginger beer), a non-alcoholic, refreshingly unsweet drink which, like cricket, is one of the few enduring British legacies to Corfiot life. Just one brewery in Kalafatiónes still makes it.

Afternoon at the Beach

Bear right along Emmanouíl Theotóki Street now, staying close to the water, and you come at once to the little waterfront eating and swimming club called **Mon Repos** (daily 8am–10pm; entrance fee), which has changing rooms, showers, toilets, beach umbrellas and sunbeds. The little beach can be busy in high season, but is less crowded in late afternoon. (The environs of Mon Repos comprise the site of ancient Corcyra, the ruins of an early Christian church and the 1824 villa where Britain's Prince Philip was born in 1921.)

After your swim, either stop off at the Nautilus, or save yourself for La Famiglia. A relative newcomer among Kérkyra's fine Italian restaurants, **La Famiglia** (30 Maniarízi keh Arlióti Street, in Kandoúni Bízi district; tel: 26610 30270) features spectacular pasta dishes such as seafood linguine, with fresh mature mussels and *vongole* (baby mussels); rigatoni with chicken sautéed in sweet wine and herbs; an antipasto salad with bruschetta; fresh vegetable quiches; and a devilish array of house desserts.

From Kapodhistríou Street, turn into Nikifórou Theotóki Street and proceed west for about three blocks, turning right into Maniarízi keh Arlióti Street: La Famiglia is just the toss of a bread roll uphill. If it is fully booked, an excellent alternative is the traditional taverna **O Yiannis** (43 Agíon Iásonos and Sosipátrou Street; tel: 26610 31066; daily 7pm–midnight, closed Sun) in the Anemomílos Quarter. Open since the late 1970s at this location, a block east of Corfu's only extant Byzantine church, dedicated to SS Jason and Sosipater, O Yiannis has preserved the time-honoured traditions of Greek tavernas of the early 20th century. You troop off to the kitchen to be shown the contents of up to two dozen 23-litre (5-gallon) cooking pots, each containing an aromatic Greek or Corfiot speciality. You make your choices – a daunting task – and sit down to such delights as veal in lemon sauce, stuffed cabbage leaves, *tsigarellí* (piquant Corfiot greens), anchovies, *bourdéto* (spicy fish soup), *sofríto* (veal in vinegar sauce), etc. This attractive, humble garden restaurant is known to everyone on the island.

At the day's end, you may want to buy a soft ice-cream cone from Igloo (48 Kapodhistríou Street) and find a seat on the Spianádha near the bandstand. The whole of Kérkyra gathers here of a summer's night until very, very late, and it's a supremely romantic place to sit under a sky that's full of twinkling stars and wheeling swallows.

2. PALACE AND NEW FORTRESS *(see map, p20–1)*

This itinerary begins with breakfast at the Art Café and Bar, then takes you to the island capital's Municipal Gallery, the Byzantine Museum and Church of Panaghía Andivouniótissa, the New Fortress and, finally, Vídhos islet, for lunch and an afternoon swim.

Start at the Art Café and Bar, in the gardens adjacent to the Municipal Gallery, at around 9.30am on any weekday but Monday. Go protected against the sun, and carry bathing gear, unless you plan to stop at your lodgings prior to the trip out to Vídhos islet.

Have breakfast in the **Art Café and Bar** gardens (tel: 26610 49366), situated to the right of the Palace of St Michael and St George, as you face it, overlooking St Nicholas Bay. Afterwards, walk round to the front of the palace and enter Kérkyra's **Municipal Art Gallery** (Dhimotikí Pinakothíki; tel: 26610 48690; daily 9am–9pm; entrance fee). In the gallery book shop you could pick up a copy of local author John Forte's *The Palace of St Michael and St George*, an entertaining history of this remarkable building.

First, enter the series of small rooms that contain travelling exhibitions of small-scale art works – often etchings, lithographs and photographs. Then, retaining your entrance ticket, retrace your steps to the Art Café and Bar gardens and enter the picture gallery up a double flight of stone steps. Just below the café here, down a sinuous iron staircase, is a nice

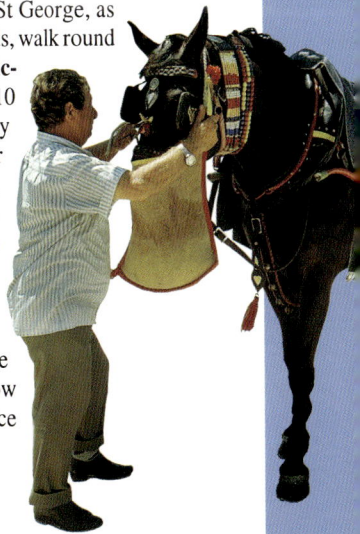

Left: soaking up the sun
Right: lunch is in the bag

Elisabeth commissioned from the German sculptor Ernst Herther in 1884, and the monumental *Achilles Triumphant*, with its gold-plated spear and helmet, an over-the-top bronze by German sculptor Johannes Gotz. The kaiser's inscription, removed by the French during World War II, read: 'This man, Achilles, son of Peleus, was erected by Germany's Wilhelm, for future generations to remember.'

The gardens, now largely closed to the public, are redolent of forsythia, jasmine and magnolia. From the portico, lined with unremarkable marbles depicting the Nine Muses, the Three Graces, and internationally renowned poets and playwrights, be sure to take a peek back into the Ahillíon at an immense oil (4m by 11m/13ft by 36ft) by Austrian painter Franz von Match depicting Achilles dragging the body of Troy's Prince Hector around the city's walls. One of the grand moments of Homer's *Iliad*, the scene certainly shows the Argives' champion, Achilles, at his best – and worst.

By Bus to the Beach

A kiosk located at the downhill end of a row of tatty tourist shops sells tickets for the Gastoúri-Kérkyra bus. Ask for directions to the bus stop and departure times for the No 10 blue bus (tickets are very reasonably priced for all island bus routes). Alternatively, taxis regularly deposit visitors at the Ahíllion, and are only too happy to find a return fare to town. Ask for Platía Saróko (San Rocco Square). The bus or taxi will leave you in town at the main blue bus terminus on Yeorghíou Theotóki, or San Rocco Square.

If you do not have your bathing gear, or are hungry, you may choose to return to your lodgings now, and/or break for lunch. The Rex or the Aegli restaurants, both located on Kapodhistríou Street behind the Listón, are both excellent choices at midday.

Return to San R0cco Square and ask for directions to the No 7 bus stop (tickets are available at a kiosk on the square). The No 7 blue bus for Dhassiá leaves about every 20 minutes from San Rócco, passing small seaside tourist hotels, olive groves and grand resorts on its 25-minute journey north. The area immediately north of Kérkyra is heavily developed, as is the seaside resort

village of **Dhassiá** itself (this is the location of the Club Mediterranée). The bus stops just outside the Elea Beach Hotel. Facing the hotel, proceed left down a paved road for about 45m (150ft), then turn sharply right down a gravel path to the beach. About 1.5km (1 mile) of pebbled beach, dotted with cafés and bars, watersport piers and umbrella and sunbed vendors awaits you. It's often more peaceful towards the far left, the Club Med end of the beach.

When you've had enough of sun and sea, retrace your steps to the Dhassiá bus stop and head back into town.

4. KANONI AND MOUNT PANDOKRATOR *(see map, p36)*

The day begins with a little jaunt by taxi, on foot and by ferry boat or caïque to the little 'suburb' of Kanóni, the church and monastery of Panaghía Vlahernón and Pondikoníssi, or 'Mouse Island'. Later, we take an afternoon-into-sunset journey by hire car to the mountain and monastery named for the Pandokrátor, or the Ruler of All.

To starting point: parking is a problem near to the starting point, so arrange to pick up a hire car later in the afternoon, and then take a taxi from Kérkyra to Kanóni. Ask to be let out at the Kafeneion (café) Kanoni. Wear comfortable shoes and modest dress, and take along beach gear and sun protection if you leave early enough to fit in a swim off Pondikoníssi.

Kanóni gets its name from an iron cannon *(kanóni)* left behind here by the French army (not the cannon that now sits in front of the café, which is Russian and only a few decades old). The hamlet is on a promontory overlooking the Halkiópoulos Lagoon and the two islets of Vlahérna and Pondikoníssi,

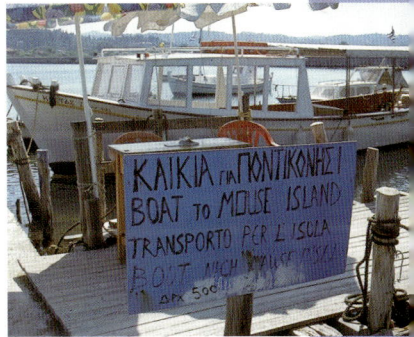

the former islet being the hallmark Corfiot image burned on the memory of every visitor to this island since the 1960s. Behind the open-air café – which you'll need to walk through – a flight of marble steps leads down to the jetty connecting Vlahérna islet to Corfu proper. Your descent takes all of three minutes, but it's slippery.

Miracle of the Virgin
Built in 1685, the tiny church and monastery of **Panaghía Vlahernón**, with its pretty Venetian belfry, is named for its miracle-working icon of the Virgin. Legend has it that Mary appeared in a dream to a Corfiot man, telling

Left: lightly tanned at Dhassiá. **Above:** the church and monastery of Panaghía Vlahernón. **Right:** boat to Pondikoníssi

Eastern Corfu

3 km / 2 miles

Itinerary 4
Itinerary 7
Itinerary 10

him that her icon had been stolen from a famous church dedicated to her in Constantinople, then left in or lost off the coast of Corfu. The man awoke, retrieved the icon, and a church was duly erected, with the same name as the icon's 5th-century Byzantine mother-church in what is today Istanbul. The Virgin's icon is festooned with *támmata* – gold, silver and tin votive offerings, left by the faithful in gratitude for answered prayers. Go in, see the icon, make a small donation, and light a beeswax candle, leaving it in the candle stand. Only one monk makes his home here now, and he's not much in evidence.

Back on the narrow concrete causeway, you will see little ferries and caïques leaving, every half hour or so in high season, for tiny **Pondikoníssi**, with its 11th- to 12th-century Byzantine **Church of the Pandokrátor**. It's a pleasant, 10-minute crossing out to the islet in the bay, where you can peek inside the church, or have a dip in the sea if you wish. Lamentably, Corfu's airport, adjacent to Kanóni, has permanently shattered the peace of this once-silent corner of the island.

Proceed back up the marble steps to the **Kafeneion Kanoni** (tel: 26610 39743; open all day), in business here since 1864, and a good place to stop for a *frappé* (iced coffee) and a slice of *sokolattína* (chocolate torte) to fortify you for the journey to Mount Pandokrátor. Incidentally, just uphill from the café is the Corfu Holiday Palace Hotel, which houses the island's only casino, should you wish to return here much, much later for less spiritual pursuits. You will need to hail a taxi and return to town to pick up your hire car a couple of hours before sunset.

Monastery on the Roof of the Island

In your hire car, leave Kérkyra via the New Port, initially following signings for Paleokastrítsa, which will take you north. After about 10km (6 miles), turn right for Dhassiá and Kassiópi. After another 2km (1¼ mile), you will pass the seaside resort town of Dhassiá and the Club Mediterranée, then immediately afterwards the busy resort of Ýpsos, directly on the sea. After 2.5km (1½ miles), turn sharply left for Spartýlas.

From here spectacular views open along the length of the east coast of Corfu, and you will drive past many private villas (including the inexplicably named Villa Hermaphrodite), but make sure you save some film for the summit. You will need to watch out for opposing traffic on this narrow, winding road (it's probably a good idea to hoot your horn approaching the blind, narrow curves). Drystone walls abound here, and olive trees seem to grow out of solid rock, standing on tiptoes of root.

In about 4km (2½ miles), after passing a roadside shrine on your right, you will enter the 'vertical village' of Spartýlas. Look for, and then follow signs, initially for the Monastery of Pandokrátoros Ypsiloú, and then for the

Right: a monk's perspective

villages of Petalía (7km/4¼ miles) and Láfki (12km/7½ miles). The views broaden as you approach the treeline, and a transmitting station looms on your left to remind you that you are in the 21st century. For a stretch here, some 30km (18 miles) from Kérkyra, views of the coastline open, and the landscape below is washed with every green in a summer painter's palette.

On top of the island, about 500m (¼ mile) further on, you enter a lovely high meadow ringed by peaks, with a 19th-century church off to your right. Stop to enjoy (but not to pick!) the wildflowers here, in season. Pass through the village of Strinýlas (make a note of the Elm Tree Taverna for dinner later), heading slightly downhill, following signs on the right for the monastery. Ahead of you now you will see the island's military listening station and its mast (Eiffel Tower as rendered by El Greco) atop the massif. The temperature drops as you ascend, traversing the vast rock garden, studded with odoriferous goats, that is the the roof of Corfu. Approaching the rocky summit, you'll see buildings rising out of the grey stone. Albania, vast and denuded, appears on your left.

At 917m (3,008ft) the **Monastery of Pandokrátoros Ypsiloú**, originally dating from the 16th century, coexists somewhat incongruously with the red-and-white radio tower, but enjoys views of all Corfu, the Dhiapóndia islets far to the west, Albania and Greek Epirus. The intimate space of the main church is filled with frescoes and 14th-century icons and has an impressive, silver-chased 18th-century iconostasis. The interior is more interesting than the bland exterior implies, so go in and have a look round. Outside the monastery gate is the Café Snack Bar Pantokrator – a bit profane, perhaps, but a welcome retreat from the sun and wind, and it does have a magnificent view.

Now retrace your route down the mountain to Strinýlas and the **Elm Tree Taverna** (tel: 26630 71454; daily 8am–midnight). Run by the Koskinas family, this excellent taverna specialises in grilled meats from the mainland city of Ioánnina – *sofríto*, and wild boar *stifádo*. Don't miss the wines, produced and bottled by the family. Next to the Elm Tree, call in at a little gift shop called The Olive Wood, also run by the Koskinas family. Here you'll find cutting boards, spoons, beads – even ersatz American-Indian dreamcatchers – all made from olive wood. Head downhill and back to Kérkyra, following all signs for the town as you go.

5. THE CAMPIELLO QUARTER *(see map, p20)*

This walking tour takes in the churches and squares of the quaint, colourful, centuries-old Campiello Quarter of Kérkyra.

Starting point: the corner of Nikifórou Theotóki and Kapodhistríou streets.

The historic town's main thoroughfare, connecting the Old and New Fortresses, is **Nikifórou Theotóki Street**. It also leads west to one of the four main entrances to the Venetian town, the Spilia Gate. (The other surviving portal through the great Venetian double walls is the St Nicholas Gate, located at Faliráki, or 'Bánio tou Alékou', beneath the Old Fortress on the sea.)

Proceed west on Nikifórou Theotóki Street. No 10 was the birthplace of two prominent Corfiots: Andreas Marmoras, a great local historian, in the 17th century, and George Theotokis, who was prime minister of Greece in the first decade of the 20th century. Today, the building is home to one of the island's oldest and most famous marching bands, the Philharmonic Society. On the right, in this first long block, is the **Church of ton Xenón** (Virgin of the Foreigners) and on the left, the **Church of Panaghía Ághios Ioánnis** (St John the Baptist). Both churches are basilicas, with three naves. At St John's, behind glass in the wall, there is a much-kissed icon depicting the Dormition of the Virgin.

The little square in front of Panaghía ton Xenón is known either as **Platía Yeorghíou Theotóki**, or the Square of the Heroes of the Cypriot Struggle. (It is also a *plakádho*, in Corfiot dialect the kind paved with marble paving stones; those paved with beach stones are called *kovoládho*.) The statue in the square, festooned with pigeons, is of George Theotokis. Proceed west, passing, at No 32, the **Papayeorghis Shop**, which sells traditional sweets and liqueurs, such as *mandóles*, *mandoláto* and kumquat liqueurs and preserves: stop and make a purchase to nibble on now or to take home as a gift. Look up now, on your right, at No 31, an old Venetian structure that has survived here for five

centuries. In the small, dead-end street just beyond No 31, the British author Lawrence Durrell resided for part of his Corfiot stay (between 1935 and 1939).

Saintly Devotion and Pagan Superstition

Look up again, at the junction of four streets, for three hanging and/or painted *pínia* (pine cones). This area, called Pínia, was the centre of the old Venetian town. According to tradition, pines and pine cones are sacred to St Spyrídhon *(see page 16)*, and the first families of Corfu displayed pine cones outside their homes to demonstrate their love for their island's patron saint. At the corner of Nikifórou Theotóki and Aghías Varváras streets is the Church of SS

Left: view from Mount Pandokrátor
Right: window on the world

Basil and Stephen. The building opposite the church is ornamented with *maskerónia*, or *mouryónia* – masks which, according to an ancient Roman custom, warded off evil. This building was part of the vast holdings of the Cobici family. A side entrance at No 3 Maniarízi keh Arlióti also has a pine cone. There are also two good restaurants in this street: Le Quattro Stagioni, at No 16, and La Famiglia, at No 30.

A tiny alley that leads down on your right now was the well-trodden route to the famous early 20th-century house of ill repute, **Lemoniá**. This block, beyond Maniarízi keh Arlióti Street, was built by the British, but in the old Venetian style. The second short street leads to the square of Lemoniá, with its lemon and mulberry trees. This area was largely razed by the Germans in World War II.

Near the west end of Nikifórou Theotóki Street, up a little flight of stairs behind an ornate wrought iron gate, is the Roman Catholic **Church of St Francis** (Ághios Frargískas). Step up into the little exterior courtyard and look at the clever drainage system here: one of the town's largest cisterns is located just below you. At the end of the street, on the right, is the town's oldest church, **Ághios Andónios** (St Anthony's), dating from the mid-16th century. An old Corfiot saying went, 'Only the old recall the sea at St Anthony's' because, in the 15th century, the sea did indeed reach this point in the town.

Turn right in front of the church into a continuation of Nikifórou Theotóki Street. On your left was the boundary of the Jewish ghetto in Venetian times (and the entrance to the New Fortress). Since the Nazi deportation of 1944 the community numbers barely 50, and the **Scuola Greca** synagogue surviving at Velissaríou is seldom used. Straight ahead now is the **Spilia Gate**, the *Pórta Spiliá*. If you're lucky, you'll hear the Third Philharmonic Society practising their brass band music near here. Within the gate proper is a little shrine to the Virgin which contains an icon that is said to work miracles.

Old Port and the Sea Walls

Head northeast and you will find yourself on Donzelót Street, in the Old Port locality. Turn right, passing the Hotel Konstantinoupolis, built in 1859 and, at No 1, the modern *Efetió* or Courthouse. Continue around the port on Donzelót Street and on your right, a block south, you will arrive at Corfu's Greek Orthodox **Cathedral (Mitrópoli)**, dedicated to the Panaghía Spiliótissa (The Virgin of the Cave) and St Theodora (the Empress of Byzantium). The Cathedral houses the headless relics of St Theodora – on her name day, the Corfiots celebrate by eating watermelon, as they believe this will somehow assist their decapitated Theodora through some form of sympathetic magic.

ΓΕΩΡΓΙΟΣ ΘΕΟΤΟΚΗΣ

Top: festooned with washing. **Left:** George Theotokis commemorated in his own square. **Right:** two demure faces of Catholic Corfu

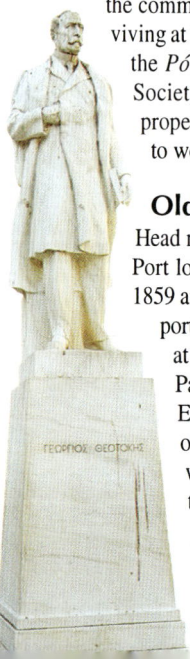

The area north of the Cathedral, towards the sea, is known as **Mourághia** (Embankments), as the Venetian fortification indeed formed sea walls here, extending east to Faliráki. The **Café Yiali** (6 Patriárhou Athinagóra Street; tel: 26610 25650) makes a romantic spot from which to view the sunset over the **Old Port**; stop here for refreshments. Climb up some steps to Donzelót Street and turn back into the Campiello Quarter via the little alleyway called Ypapandís Street. Turn immediately left here and on your left you will see a lovely stone balcony and a tiny square – 3rd Párodhos Ypapandís Square (*párodhos* means alleyway); then comes 4th Párodhos Ypapandís Street. Here you can see the remains of more **Venetian walls**. Here, too, once stood the house of Dionysios Solomos, who wrote Greece's national anthem.

Proceed gently uphill and east, parallel to the Mouráyia. Turn right into 4th Párodhos Arseníou Street, and examine the typical, tall, Venetian-style buildings here. The true Venetian structures have very low portals and defensive window shutters. Look up at the centuries-old clothes-drying system still utilised here, whereby clothes lines are strung between the windows of facing buildings.

Take the first left and then immediately go right under a series of arches. The exterior staircases and *foursoúsia* – stone yard-arms from which planters of flowers were hung by the Venetians – are characteristic of the quarter. You will now enter a little square with a lone palm tree. Cross the square towards a raspberry-hued building behind the palm. Turn left, passing the Crêperie/Wine Bar Campiello on your right, then turn right at the corner and head down the steps to the **Square of Kremastí** (Suspended One). The church here is called the Panaghía Kremastí (Suspended Virgin). There are two explanations for this name: either it derives from an icon of the Virgin or Christ on the Cross that was displayed here, or the Venetians used this square for executions. Today, the excellent **Venetian Well** restaurant dominates the square.

Leaving Platía Kremastí, with the Venetian Well restaurant on your right, proceed downhill on 4th Párodhos Komninón Street. Turn right into Aghías Theodhóras Street, where you will see above you more *fouroúsia*, then high corbelled arches and, on your left, a solitary *maskaróni* embedded into a house

reputed to have once belonged to John Kapodhistrias. Turn left into Filel-línon Street, today a busy tourist shopping thoroughfare. At No 18 stands the mid-17th-century house of the Mastrakas family, with its carved portal and beautiful balconies. The entire street is *plakádho*, paved in marble paving stones. Turn right into 3rd Párodhos Arlióti Street, and you are back at the La Famiglia restaurant. From here wend your way downhill back to Nikifórou Theotóki Street, and you're back where you began.

6. BY HYDROFOIL TO PAXI *(see map, p43)*

This is a day-long excursion by hydrofoil to the idyllic nearby island of Paxí.

To the starting point: The night prior to your departure have your hotel desk arrange for a taxi to take you to the hydrofoil quay in Kérkyra's New Port. The hydrofoil for the islands of Paxí and Andípaxi leaves early, between 7 and 8.30am depending on the day of the week. Take along sun protection and beach gear – and your driving licence, in case you decide to hire a car for the day.

Purchase a return ticket (approx. €18) on the quay, and be sure to board the right hydrofoil for Paxí – several hydrofoils operate from this quay and it's easy to board the wrong craft. Also be sure, once you arrive on Paxí, to enquire about the hydrofoil's precise return time in the late afternoon.

The journey from Kérkyra to the port of Gaïos on Paxí takes about an hour, unless – as sometimes happens – there's a detour to Igoumenítsa. Only sailboats and small launches dock at Gaïos proper, passing through the fjord-like entry channel. Hydrofoils dock 1km (½ mile) away, from where you can either take the scenic, shoreline walk or catch a taxi into the town.

Gaïos is a busy, charming, human-scaled port on tiny Paxí, a place that still looks like a proper Greek island town should. In fact, all of Paxí seems dedicated to the azure sea and the olive, as opposed to the acquisition of foreign currency. Stop anywhere at any of the cafés on the main square, near the Church of the Annunciation, for morning coffee. The soft seats of the Center Snack Bar (tel: 26620 32698; daily) are an inviting place to take the weight off your feet.

At the National Bank of Greece branch (which doubles as a hardware store), located behind Gaïos's fish market, just off the square, pick up a copy of poet/historian/banker Spiros H Bogdanos's *Paxoi: From Yesterday to Today* for a little précis

Above: swimming off Paxí

on Paxí and Andípaxi. A bit further down this narrow, unnamed street is Litsa and Marina Petsalis's little gift shop, **Silvereyes** (tel: 26620 32381), which sells unusual handcrafted gifts: beach stones with painted eyes 'against the Evil Eye', and olive wood ships.

Now ask to be directed to Gaïos Travel, where you can hire a car from Mr Yannis Arvanitakis (tel: 26620 32033/31651/ 32506; fax: 26620 32175; or e-mail: gaiostrv@otenet.gr; or contact his website: www.gaiostravel.com). After that, simply set out to explore the island, from Gaïos to Fondána to Longós to Lákka. There are two attractive little beachlets – Kamína and Kakí Langádha – just north of Gaïos. At the beginning and end of the season, you will have them to yourself.

It's only 6.5km (4 miles) from here to the pretty port town of **Longós**, where you can walk to Levréhio beach. By far the best restaurant in Longós is **Vassilis**, at the narrowest point of the quay (tel: 26620 31587). Here, too, with its incomparable, dreamlike sea view, is the Café Bar To Taxidi (tel: 26620 31326; Easter–Oct, daily 1pm–2am).

Some 4km (2½ miles) further north is the port of **Lákka**, with a yacht marina, beaches and shops. **La Rosa di Paxos** (tel: 26620 31471), a bar and restaurant run by Italian Cinzia Casalini and her Greek husband, Michaelis Dalietos, is a great place to sample 'Levantine specialities' from Spain, Italy, Greece and Morocco – for a special splurge, with a wine list to match. Stop in, too, at **Il Pareo** (tel: 26620 30046), which stocks Far Eastern clothing, accessories, linens and, not surprisingly, an astonishing array of *pareos*.

If you want to visit Andípaxi, you can arrange transport through Gaïos Travel, but you will not be able to get back to Corfu the same day. Should you decide to stay on Paxí overnight, or want to come back for a longer stay, Ms Vassiliki Malamas's **Pithari Villas** (Gaïos, Paxos, 49082, Greece; tel/fax: 26620 32491; in Athens, tel: 210 6817025) make a wonderful place to stay, only 50m/yds from the marina (*see page 90*).

Paxí and Andípaxi

5 km / 3 miles

(*see page 90*)

Above: the owners of Il Pareo

7. AGHIOS STEFANOS SINION AND AGNI *(see map, p36)*

A sybaritic and gastronomic itinerary by rented car to the picturesque beach hamlets of Ághios Stéfanos Sinión and Agní, for sunbathing, boating, swimming – and especially for fine cuisine.

To the starting point: leave Kérkyra via the New Port, and head north following signs for Kassiópi all the way up Corfu's northeast coast. After about 30km (18 miles) turn right at signs for Ághios Stéfanos Sinión. To reach Agní later on, you will have to get back on the main road and proceed south for some 5km (3 miles) before turning left down a poor secondary road for Agní Beach.

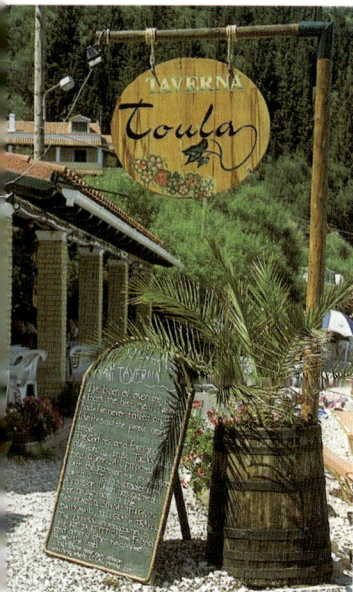

One of several Corfiot towns named after St Stephen (to whom Corfu's first Christian church was dedicated), **Ághios Stéfanos Sinión** is a beautiful, peaceful little fishing village on a minute stretch of beach, just north of Jacob Rothschild's Corfiot hideaway. Stop on the pebbled beach for a swim, and have a bite to eat at the **Eucalyptus** (tel: 26630 82007; May–Oct, 8am–late), perhaps pan-fried or grilled whitebait or red mullet. There are a couple of nice bars here as well – should you decide to stay over and be looking for something to do in the evening.

Ághios Stéfanos is frequented by small yacht flotillas in season, and you can hire small motorboats on the beach and visit nearby beachlets inaccessible except by sea. (Albania is a stone's throw away from the Corfiot coast here, but *do not* attempt to land there.) If the place takes your fancy, go along to the **Kochili Restaurant** (tel: 26630 81522/81886) at the southern end of the beach. Helen and Yerasimos Tsirimiagos rent rooms and apartments, and should be able to find you a place to stay at short notice, except at the height of the season. Helen, the cook at the Kochili, produces excellent oven-baked fresh anchovies, and *skorpios* fish in lemon sauce, plus homemade crêpes, savoury and sweet. Alternatively, between Ághios Stéfanos Sinión and Kerasiá (the next beach down the coast) Mr Theophanis Hondroyannis has a few apartments to rent in an idyllic olive grove (Aliki Apartments; tel: 26630 81966 or 26610 4856).

Now, if you've had a swim and a light lunch at Ághios Stéfanos Sinión, and are heading back to Kérkyra around dinnertime, turn left off the main Kérkyra road after about 12km (7½ miles) and proceed for 3km (2 miles) to tiny **Agní Beach**, where you will find two of the island's best tavernas.

Right on the pebble beach is **Toula** (tel: 26630 91350; 10am–5pm, 7–11pm in season), which has been owned and operated by Ms Toula Vergheti since 1982. Before that the building was an olive press belonging to Toula's father. Justly renowned in the foreign press for her prawns and mussels, Toula also concocts fabulous chocolate crêpes. Next door is the **Taverna Agni** (tel: 26630 91142; e-mail agnitave@otenet.gr), which is even more famous abroad

Above: come to Toula for prawns and mussels and great chocolate crêpes
Right: the cliffs at Sidhári

due to the international love story of its proprietors (he is British, she is Corfiot). Try the king prawn *saganaki*, Eleni's garlic prawns, or lamb pie – and finish up with a glass of port, with Stilton and Carr's water biscuits.

8. BY CAIQUE TO ERIKOUSSA ISLET *(see map, p46)*

This excursion, by hire car then caïque or ferry, takes in the north-western resort town of Sidhári and the Dhiapóndian islet of Eríkoussa, where you can enjoy a swim and a bracing walk round the islet.

To the starting point: well in advance of your voyage, call Mr Phillip Vlasseros (Vlasseros Travel, Sidhári; tel: 26630 95695) to arrange caïque or ferry trans-port to Eríkoussa. He will hold tickets for you at his travel agency, to be collected on the morning of your journey (Mr Vlasseros usually walks his clients out to the quay and sees them aboard the right craft). Hire a car in Kérkyra and set out early for the 37-km (23-mile) drive to Sidhári, leaving town via the Old and the New Port. Take beach gear and sun protection, drinking water bottles, fruit and snacks – preferably in a backpack.

Leave town to the west, then north, using Dhimokratías Avenue. Pass the Old Fortress, then drive through the portico/colonnade of the Palace of St Michael and St George. Dhimokratías soon metamorphoses into Ars-eníou Street, then Donzelót Street, then Zavitsianoú Street. Hug the bay, pass-ing the New Fortress on your left. Ferries and hydrofoils leave the Old Port quays here for Italy, the Greek mainland and Paxí. Follow signs for Pale-okastrítsa. You will be retracing the blue bus route to Dhassiá *(see page 32)*, until you turn off to the west at Tzavarátika. Then bear right, follow-ing signs for Sidhári, and pass through the village of Skriperó, with Mt Pan-dokrátor on your right. The road winds up above the olive-carpeted valley. At the village of Troumbétas (Trumpet), cross the spine of Pandokrátor, and begin your descent to the northern coast of the island.

You pass through several hillside hamlets until the road drops to the littoral and you enter the resort of **Sidhári**. Drive through the town, keeping

close to the shore, and turn right at The Three Little Pigs Restaurant. At Maria's Restaurant/Cocktail Bar you have access to Sidhári's once-pristine beach and the famous **Canal d'Amour** area of dramatically eroded headlands.

Sidhári has succumbed to tourist tat. It's a 'chips with everything' sort of place in high season, but you may choose to have a swim here another time. If you arrive having skipped breakfast, stop at Costa's Bakery (tel: 26630 95121) on the main strip, for a croissant or cheese pie.

Across the Water to Eríkoussa

Having prearranged your boat trip with Mr Vlasseros, you will be taking a caïque or ferry to Eríkoussa (sometimes written Erikoússa) islet, one of the three small **Dhiapóndia** islets 11 sea miles northwest of Corfu. Inhabited by some 150 Corfiot-Americans, who made their fortunes in the United States, then repatriated, Eríkoussa has its own mayor and school but, for the most part, its young people return to Astoria in New York City for the winter. There are two places to stay: the **Erikoussa Hotel** (tel: 26630 71555), and rooms at the **Anemomylos Taverna** (tel: 26630 71647).

Look for the offices of Vlasseros Travel on Sidhári's tourist strip. Mr Phillip Vlasseros is an English-speaking authority on the Dhiapóndia islets. He can also arrange accommodation in private villas. If you do stay in the area, note that

Northern Corfu

5 km / 3 miles

Itinerary 8
Itinerary 12
Itinerary 17

2km (1¼ miles) west of Sidhári is the village of Perouládhes and cliff-bottom Sunset Beach, a nice place to swim and enjoy the beautiful sunset behind the Dhiapóndia islands. There's also a wide, sandy beach at **Ághios Stéfanos Avliotón**, 10km (6 miles) southwest of Sidhári, a package-tour centre where there are restaurants and rooms to let galore (*not* Ághios Stéfanos Sinión, covered on page 44). The northern end of this crescent-shaped beach is cleanest. Five minutes' walk west of the beach is a tiny caïque harbour; swimming off the rocks beyond the harbour beats braving the hordes on the beach in July.

The voyage to **Eríkoussa** (daily except Tues, departure 9.30am in high season; return 4pm) takes just under an hour. Of the three Dhiapóndia islets, Eríkoussa is the easternmost (Mathráki is furthest south and closest to Corfu, with a fabulous, long beach; Othoní is westernmost and is fairly inaccessible). Eríkoussa, where the former US President George Bush visited by helicopter, and Prince Charles by yacht, is as quiet as Corfu's northwest coast is noisy. Keeping an eye on your watch, set out on foot to ramble the island's peripheral roads: there's a simple map posted at the end of the jetty.

Garden Attractions

Eríkoussa is an underpopulated flower, fruit and vegetable garden, so just set out, and then return to the main beach (and port) to swim in clear waters before returning to Sidhári. The best place for lunch on the islet is the Hotel Erikoussa (tel/fax: 26630 71555/ 71110; May–mid-Sept, for all meals), but arrive early as when the food is gone, it's gone. The best time to photograph the Canal d'Amour is on the return voyage, when your captain will steer the boat close to the rocks, offering passengers the best photo opportunities.

Above: on the way to Eríkoussa
Right: a young passenger poses

9. ALONAKI BAY AND THE SOUTH *(see map, p49)*

This trip by hire car will take you further down Corfu's western coast, to stop at the Byzantine fortress of Gardhíki, swim off Halikoúnas Beach, view Lake Korissíon and lunch at secluded Alonáki Bay.

To the starting point: following the directions provided for Itinerary 13, proceed to the village of Sinarádhes, and then follow signs (to the right, just out of town) for Ághios Górdhis, which you reach after 3km (2 miles) of winding road. If you're going to do any walking, take sturdy shoes or hiking boots.

The western coastline is dramatic at **Ághios Górdhis**, but the beach is crowded in season, so head up and inland. After 2.5km (1½ miles) of steep and winding road, you enter the largely unspoilt farming village of Káto Garoúna. After a short distance, bear left towards Kérkyra and look out for a right turn towards Ághios Matthéos. In 3km (2 miles) you enter the village of Vouniatádhes, where every house has its own grape arbour. Some 2km (1¼ miles) further on, enter **Ághios Matthéos** and follow signs for Lefkími. This friendly, prosperous town has red-tiled buildings and a shady main street lined with cafés, should you wish to stop for a drink or an ice-cream.

About 1.5km (1 mile) from Ághios Matthéos, you'll come to a major group of signposts. Turn right for Halikoúnas and Gardhíki. After about 1km (½ mile), bear left and you will see the 13th-century Byzantine fortress of **Gardhíki** on your right. Get out and have a look inside the walls (watching out for snakes). The ruined walls here are divided into eight sections by postern towers and on an upper floor of the south tower, in what was once perhaps a chapel, are shadowy wall paintings of saints.

Drive for another 2km (1¼ miles), through silent groves, gardens and vineyards until you come to signs for Alonáki Bay, where you should bear right. The tarmac ends and the road turns to pebble, and you're entering a little corner of Corfu known only to the locals and a few visitors. Some 2km (1¼ miles) further on, turn right at signs for **Alonáki Bay**. Here is a

Above: the Alonáki Bay taverna

little taverna (tel: 26610 75872/76118; May–Oct, open all day, but phone in advance) serving local specialities – freshly caught fish, lobster and octopus, as well as shrimps from Lake Korissíon. Owned and run by Mihalis and Katerina Varagoulis and their family, the taverna comprises a few widely spaced tables sheltering beneath the low branches of stunted trees directly above the beach: heaven on earth. There are also a few rooms to let here if you feel like staying on.

Birdwatchers' Lake and Hideaway Beach

After lunch, retrace your route to the signs for Halikoúnas Beach. Turn right and proceed till the road surface turns to dirt. On your left, you will see the flat, blue waters of **Lake Korissíon**, of great interest to international birdwatchers, who have identified some 150 species of birds on the island, among them the glossy ibis, spoonbill, pygmy cormorant and great white egret. On your right is **Halikoúnas Beach** – a secret haunt of the locals until now – with its expanse of shingle and strange, sculptural pebbles. Spread out your towel and have a swim on this largely deserted, silent stretch of beach – a rare experience in the Ionian islands today.

As you retrace your route to Kérkyra, less than 1km (just over ½ mile) back up the dirt track from Halikoúnas Beach you will notice the **Rainbow Family**

Southern Corfu map

Taverna (tel: 26610 76384) on the left. This little oasis of carefully tended flowers is a pleasant place to stop (it also has pristine toilet facilities). Mr and Mrs Spyros and Eleni Armeniakos cook for visitors as though they were family, and Eleni makes a delicious cup of Greek coffee: order it sweet *(glykós)* or medium *(métrios)*. You can stop just for a cold drink or an ice-cream as well. Suitably refreshed, continue on your way, bearing right into Ághios Matthéos and Sinarádhes, following clearly marked signs for the route back to Kérkyra.

10. ALTERNATIVE CORFU *(see map, p36)*

This little chapter introduces you to the Casa Lucia cottage complex and retreat, located outside the village of Sgómbou; Medi Jeunesse, in Kérkyra, which offers myriad skin treatments and fitness classes; and Ms Vana Soueref's beauty salon.

To the starting point: Casa Lucia is 12km (7½ miles) northwest of Kérkyra by taxi or rented car. About 11km (7 miles) from town, near the village of Sgómbou, you will turn left at a little blue sign for the cottage retreat, which is clearly signed, a short distance off the main road. Both Medi Jeunesse and Vana Soueref's salon are in or near the historic centre of Kérkyra.

In order to get to know a new culture well it is important to participate in the daily life of the foreign land just as you would at home, experiencing as much as you possibly can of what the culture has to offer on a day-to-day basis. So, between visits to the beach, explore alternative healing and meditation at Casa Lucia, take an aerobics class at Medi Jeunesse with young Greek instructors who speak very little English, and have Ms Vana Soueref style your hair – your stay will be so much the richer for it.

   Casa Lucia (Sgómbou; tel: 26610 91419; fax: 26610 91732; e-mail: ganders@otenet.gr) was established by Mr and Mrs Dennis and Val Androut-sopoulos in 1977. Today, the cottage complex comprises 11 bungalows,

which are let out to visitors on a daily basis between Easter and the end of October, with maid service, swimming pool, welcome pack and other perks in high season; in winter, self-catering visitors may book accommodation by the week or the month.

Casa Lucia is a little paradise of meditative healing, the cottages set in a series of tailored gardens, but the remarkable facets of a stay here are the alternative healing and creative arts seminars, with sessions and workshops throughout the year. Do fax Val direct – Corfiot e-mail is an uncertain proposition, still – and she will supply you with a schedule of upcoming events. Book in advance if you want to visit in high season, though Val says that even if you show up unexpectedly, she often has a free cottage.

Your stay might coincide with a Tai Chi session and a mini-course in Sacred Circle dance. Other recent offerings have included a weekend-long Buddhist meditation retreat, reiki at all three levels of mastery, shiatsu, aromatherapy, reflexology, acupuncture and herbal therapy treatments, Swedish massage, manicures and pedicures, and creative writing and poetry workshops.

At the end of the day, you can walk out to the main road to **La Lucciola Taverna** (Sgómbou; tel: 26610 90821) an excellent Italian bistro-in-a-garden run by Mr and Mrs Peppino and Lory Nava, of Napoli. Eat some delicious, sophisticated pasta under the pines there, and listen to the cries of the Scops and little owls before driving back into town. It's a great place to eat if you do decide to take a weekend course or spend a few nights at the Casa Lucia.

The Body Beautiful

Back in Kérkyra, there are other notable oases of pampering. Ms Areti Kourkoulou's **Medi Jeunesse** (16 Ioánni Andreádhi Street; tel: 26610 43434/44475; also at 18 Spýrou Kondomári Street, off San Rócco Square; tel: 26610 25616/28030) offers fine skin treatments, as well as a plethora of fitness classes. Have your hotel desk book, say, a facial with Ms Kourkoulou herself, then proceed by taxi to her salon on San Rocco.

For women's and men's hair treatments – and outstanding cuts – Ms Vana Soueref's salon **Kommoteirio** (1 Dhelvinióti Street; tel: 26610 38362), located behind the old-town branch of the National Bank of Greece, is a pleasant place to have one's saltwater-stressed locks trimmed, shorn, styled, coloured or permed. Ms Soueref's English is minimal, which doesn't bother her international clientele in the least. Everyone goes out looking terrific! Have your hotel make your appointment in advance and explain exactly what services you want. (The reasonable prices for all aesthetic services on Corfu will be another nice surprise.)

Left: Tai Chi in motion
Above: in a whirl in the jacuzzi at Casa Lucia

12. ANGELOKASTRO AND PALEOKASTRITSA
(see map, p46)

This excursion by hire car takes you to the 12th-century castle of Angelókastro, atop its dizzy precipice above the sea, near the village of Kríni; and to the beautiful, bustling resort town of Paleokastrítsa, where you visit the 13th-century Monastery of the Holy Virgin.

To the starting point: follow the same route as for Itinerary 8 (see page 45), as far as the village of Troumbétas, then follow directions below. Take along beach gear, but wear very modest clothing for your visit to the monastery – and you'll need sturdy walking shoes.

At Troumbétas, rather than head over the pass and down to the northwest littoral, follow signs for Alimatádhes and Vístonas. As you climb, you will

have dramatic views to the northwest and east, taking in the Dhiapóndia islets and Albania. Some 3km (2 miles) out of Troumbétas, go straight on, ignoring a sign on the right for Alimatádhes. The heights here are rich in grapes and olives and yellow with flowering broom in spring.

After 4.5km (3 miles), you pass through the village of Vístonas, with its olive oil presses and a delightful roadside stand called **The Mulberry Tree** (tel: 26630 49049). An Englishwoman called Joy runs this concern, along with her father-in-law, Mr Spyros Konstandis, as an outlet for the family's own range of wines, honey and olive oil, as well as hand-crafted lace and olive-wood bowls and implements.

Dramatic Vistas

As you head out of Vístonas, Angelókastro (Angel Castle) appears directly before you, looking for all the world like a Steven Spielberg special effect, floating on a pillar of olive trees: this is perhaps the single most dramatic sight on Corfu. Follow signs for Kríni and Angelókastro (and give souvenir-hawkers a wide berth as you enter Kríni: they will actually try to flag your car down to sell you things, a rarity in Greece).

Bear to the left and pass the Panorama Café. Continue, counter-intuitively downhill, following the frequent signs for the Angelókastro. The paved road winds through olive groves, netted for the harvest which takes place from late autumn to May. You will get a superb photo opportunity 1km (½ mile) out of Kríni: pull off the road into a small gravel lay-by to take stunning shots of the castle ahead. An equal distance downhill brings you to a car park and the ticket booth for **Angelókastro** (now open again after restoration).

A Byzantine stronghold built for the 12th-century Emperor Manuel Komnenos, the castle proved to be an almost impregnable fortress and was known to the Angevins as the *Castrum Sancti Angeli*. It held out against attacks

Above: a gnarled olive tree

by pirates, the Genoese and the Ottoman Turkish invaders of Corfu, and was in use as a fortified retreat throughout the 16th century: some 300m (984ft) above the sea, with its own mighty water reservoir, Angelókastro's church was dedicated to the archangels Michael and Gabriel. (Watch attentively for snakes on your ascent to the summit: this fortress is still well guarded – but by reptiles.)

From the castle, you can see Kérkyra off in the distance to the southeast, and just about everything else in four directions. Retrace your route now to Makrádhes, where you will bear right for Lákones. Views down to the sea and the resort of Paleokastrítsa are breathtaking, but watch for oncoming traffic. The Bella Vista Grill/Bar or the Golden Fox on the road here are good places to stop, take refreshment, and savour the view. **Lákones**, which you reach after 1km (½ mile) or so, is a roadside village where elderly women in traditional, white Corfiot headscarves sit on their doorsteps and watch the passing parade. Descend sharply, then, through terraced olive groves, following signs for Paleokastrítsa.

A Monastic Haven

Paleokastrítsa, one of the island's most famous resorts, is lively and loud in high season, the traffic all but eclipsing the natural beauty of the place, which comprises dramatic azure coves, verdant promontories and intimate beaches. One area of Paleokastrítsa which retains all its beauty is the 13th-century **Monastery of the Holy Virgin** (daily 7am–1pm, 3–8pm), with its remarkable church. Home to a handful of monks and novices, some from Central Europe, this fortified eyrie has a stunning church containing icons of the Virgin to which miracles have been attributed, and a beautiful, painted, mid-18th-century iconostasis, or icon screen. The monastery gardens are verdant and peaceful and a little museum exhibits 16th- and 17th-

Above: dramatic Angelókastro
Right: Kríni villagers take a view on life

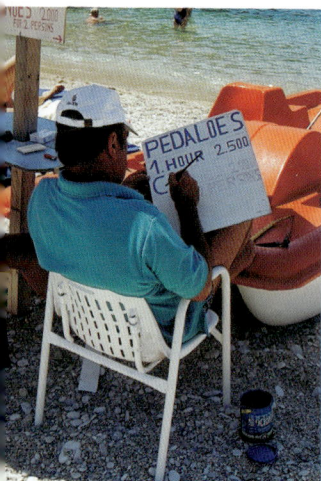

century vestments, icons and the skeleton of what residents describe as a 'sea monster', actually an unfortunate whale which was slaughtered in 1860 by French seamen. The monastery and resort celebrate three feast days – on the first Friday after Orthodox Easter, on 13 July and on 15 August – at which times it's standing room only in Paleokastrítsa.

Adjacent to the monastery is an unnamed restaurant – more a café, really – that makes a hospitable venue for light meals, snacks and drinks, all consumed among the perambulating monastery peacocks (which can never be coaxed into spreading their dizzily kaleidoscopic tails). Alternatively, on the way back out of town, at the foot of steps leading down to the sea, is the **Akron Beach Bar and Tennis Court** (tel: 26630 41226), a good place to combine lunch and/or dinner with a swim and a pricy but worthwhile trip by hired motor boat to nearby, but almost inaccessible, beaches. More committed visitors can patronise one of three local scuba schools offering dives into the habitually brisk water here.

13. FOLKLORE HERITAGE OF CORFU *(see map, p33)*

Set aside a Thursday to visit Sinarádhes folklore museum; spend the evening with dinner or just drinks by the pool at the Grecotel Corfu Imperial in Komméno, for a performance of authentic Greek dancing.

To the starting point: leave Kérkyra via the airport/Lefkími road. After less than 1km (½ mile), follow signs right for Pélekas. The road passes through Alepoú and Tríklino, where you'll see a sign for Pélekas 7km (4¼ miles). Bear left for Pélekas/Sinarádhes. In about 3km (2 miles), you'll come to a crossroads. Turn left for Sinarádhes (sign in Greek only) and, immediately, you're in the village.

In **Sinarádhes**, park near the little town square, with its lone central palm tree, and walk slightly uphill. Across from the Philharmonic Society of Sinarádhes and the Church of Ághios Nikólaos, signs to the museum will direct you up steps. Wend your way steeply uphill and left and in a short distance you will reach the **Folklore Museum of Central Corfu** (daily 9.30am–2.30pm, closed Sun and Mon; entrance fee).

The house here is typical of rural central Corfu, and dates from 1860, but since life on the island changed little over the following century the lifestyle mirrored here could just as easily represent Corfu in 1960, when

Above: peddling his wares, Paleokastrítsa
Right: dancer at the Grecotel Corfu Imperial

your author first visited the island. The simplicity – and poverty – of life for most Corfiots up until very recent times is evocatively expressed in the Spartan nature of this dwelling.

As you enter the first-floor living quarters (the ground floor is still a private residence), you see a *pithári*, which would have contained the family's year-long supply of olive oil, the staple of the Greek diet then as now. An entire family would have lived in these three sparsely furnished rooms – perhaps 10 people, who would have been out in the fields all day, coming home to roost only at night. Most rural life went on out of doors, and dwellings were simply a place for eating and sleeping.

The exhibits are well marked in English and German, and helpful staff members will tell you much about the artefacts. The kitchen, a bedroom and a 'formal' parlour or dining room (opened only for special occasions such as saints' days and engagements), comprise the home. Notice the traditional birthing chair, a type still used by some local midwives. Upstairs – where a second family would have lived – is a display of some interesting non-domestic exhibits: a primitive papyrus boat, used on the west coast of Corfu until the mid-20th century (and of a type dating back to the Egyptians); a loom; agricultural tools; a shadow puppet *(karaghiózis)* theatre; a cobbler's bench; and a potter's wheel. There's also an exhibit on Corfiot women's headscarves, each of which would have denoted the wearer's village of origin and her marital status, simply through colour and pattern.

After viewing the museum, wander around Sinarádhes for a while, to discover a farming village that still remains much as it was in 1860.

Folk Dance Evenings

Drive back to your hotel in the afternoon, have a siesta perhaps, and then don your finery and head out to Komméno and the **Grecotel Corfu Imperial** (tel: 26610 91481/2; performances Thurs 8–11.30pm, Sun 9–11.30pm). This complex, which sprawls beautifully over much of the Komméno peninsula, with spectacular gardens and superb bars and restaurants, comprises the island's finest hotel. You can sit by the pool, sip a Bellini or a beer from either the Alkinoos or Odysseus bar, and watch (or join in with) the professional troupe of traditionally costumed Greek dancers, and there's a barbecue dinner to accompany the dancing. (If you prefer your music cool, there's usually a duo playing indoors at the Art Deco-styled Alkinoos Bar.)

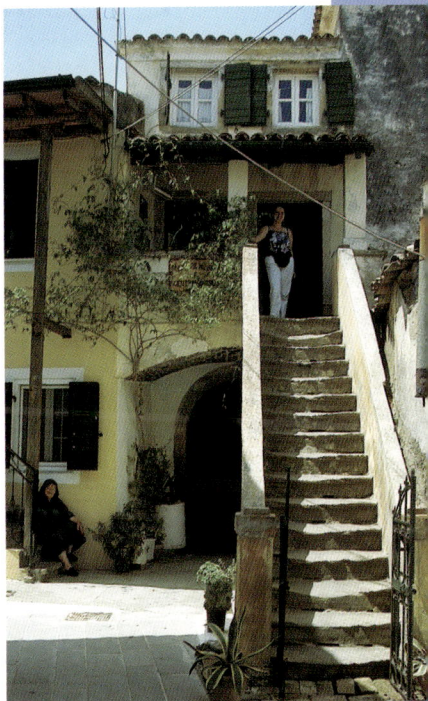

Right: to the Sinarádhes Folk Museum

Bar Supervisor Mr Alex Mortzos, who created the hotel's impressive cocktail menu, recommends something called a Grecotel Surprise in the heat of summer: 3 parts gin, 2 parts exotic fruit liqueur, 1 part Amaretto, with orange juice and strawberry syrup to fill. (Good thing you're not driving back to your lodgings.) There's also draught Mythos and Warsteiner Pils, champagne cocktails galore and Piper Heidsieck by the glass, all reasonably priced, considering this is a luxury complex.

If you prefer to dine elsewhere (and there is no hotel barbecue on Sunday), you will still have time to do this after the show. Consult the *Eating Out* section of this guide, and reserve a table for late evening. Spyros and Vasilis, or Etrusco would be good nearby choices *(see pages 72–3).*

14. Sunday in Kerkyra *(see map, p20–21)*

If religious, you could start in Kérkyra with a service at Holy Trinity Anglican Church, then take a tour of the British Cemetery, preferably in the company of Hilary Whitton Païpeti, a noted local writer and guide; spend the evening at two quintessentially Corfiot night spots – the cinema and (during the right season) the Jazz Rock Club.

To the starting point: if you want your visit to the cemetery to include the guided tour, contact Ms Païpeti (PO Box 445, Kérkyra, Corfu, 49100 Greece; tel/fax: 26610 52833; e-mail: corfiotm@otenet.gr) well in advance to make arrangements. Holy Trinity Church is just two or three blocks west of the Spianádha, a stone's throw from the Bella Venezia Hotel.

In 1864, when the British Protectorate (which is what the British occupation of Corfu was called) ended, and the Church of St George within the Old Fortress became Greek Orthodox, the Greek authorities offered the Ionian Parliament building 'to the Corfu community of the Anglican faith'. Today, **Holy Trinity Anglican Church** (21 L Mavíli Street; tel: 26610 31467; service Sun at 10.30am, 1st and 3rd Sun 7pm) is spiritual home to a diverse body of Corfiot, expatriate and visiting Christians, of all denominations and all nationalities. Regular services are conducted by the Reverend Stuart Broughton (of Cheshire) – and communion on Sunday mornings is followed by refreshments in the garden.

The church tends towards the 'happy-clappy' end of Anglicanism (you have been warned!), in a recent Pentecost, a diverse congregation of British, Irish, Albanian, Canadian, South African, American, Filipino, Ethiopian, Greek, German, Mexican, Dutch and Swiss worshippers attended a charismatic service which included modern dance, and guitar and mandolin music – with homemade brownies to follow.

Roman Catholic services are held at the **Roman Catholic Cathedral** or **Duomo of Ághios Iákovos** (Platía Dhimarhíou; May–Sept, Sat 7pm, Sun 8.30am, 10am and 7pm), and there are other Catholic services at Gozzela, in Dhassiá, and at the Catholic Camping in Messongí; check at the Duomo for hours.

Above: serving the spiritual needs of some of Corfu's expatriates
Right: the British cemetery

Garden of Peace and Poetry

The more secular-minded can take a taxi straight to Kolokotróni Street, the location of the lovely **Anglikó Nekrotafío** (British Cemetery), which dates from the years of the British Protectorate (1814–64). You don't have to take a guided tour, but it is highly recommended because Hilary Whitton Païpeti's knowledge adds so much to the experience. (You may also be interested to know that Ms Païpeti leads a variety of tours on the island, including Corfiot Wildflowers in Spring, The Durrell Tour, Picturesque Corfiot Villages and Corfiot Fortresses.) A garden full of 'English poetry' and peace on a verdant hill above the town, the cemetery has a dazzling array of Corfiot flora, both wild and cultivated, which is at its best in April or May. Botanists and gardeners from all over the world visit the British Cemetery in spring to examine over 45 types of wild orchid that bloom here.

The monuments and gravestones within these walls tell the whole history of the British on Corfu, and military historians will be fascinated by the eloquent markers dating from both world wars. As remarkable as the wildflowers and the stones is the cemetery's caretaker, Mr George Psaïlas, who was actually born and married in the cemetery, and who has already prepared his own grave and marker. A fount of information about the 'residents' of his garden, Mr Psaïlas is a sort of Corfiot historian-philosopher. Share a few moments with him in his backyard, so to speak, and wander among the evocative stones. (Mr Psaïlas is also something of a writer: ask to purchase his pair of little booklets on the cemetery and its orchids.)

When you've seen enough, turn right out of the front gate and, at the end of the block, right again into Mitropolíti Methodhíou Street. Proceed four blocks downhill to San Rocco Square. As Ms Païpeti tells her charges, this street is lined with 'real' Greek shops – hardware, hairdressers and plumbers – so you get a glimpse of Kérkyra life away from the touristic centre. On Sunday many of these workaday emporia will be closed, but shops catering for tourists, as well as cafés and restaurants, will all be open.

The Commercial Heart of Town

San Rocco Square, the 17th-century marketplace that developed outside the main gate to the old Venetian city, the Porto Reale, is noisy and congested but it's where most of the town's business takes place and where the blue-bus terminal and a taxi rank are located. Cross Alexándhras Avenue here, and go straight ahead on Yeorghíou Theotóki Street, the main modern shopping thoroughfare. Proceed three blocks further on, passing Marks & Spencer (the original location of the Porto Reale), and entering the old town near the National Bank of Greece. The Roman Catholic church here was demolished by a German bombardment during World War II.

The road changes names here, becoming Vlahióti Street. Turn left at the fountain, in a square known locally as the Piazza, into Mihaïl Theotóki Street. At the end of a short block, turn right into Nikifórou Theotóki Street and proceed east to Kapodhistríou Street and the familiar territory of the Listón. If you are hungry, the Aegli or the Rex are nearby, but you may want to return to your lodgings to freshen up, then find a place for an early dinner.

Take a taxi unless you are within walking distance, to the corner of Yerásimou Aspióti and Akadhimías streets; you may wish to pause here and spray on some mosquito repellent. Here, right in the heart of town, within a block of one another, are the summer cinema Phoenix (not to be confused with the winter cinema Orfeas, also located near here), and the Jazz Rock Garden (which also has alternative winter digs on Yerásimou Aspióti Street), two of the most popular warm-weather, after-dark venues for the locals.

Movies under the Stars

The **Summer Cinema Phoenix** (Fínikas; 1 Ioánnou Daliétou Street; tel: 26610 37482; early Jun–early Sept, 9.30pm–midnight), a 250-seat open-air cinema within a walled garden, shows recent Greek and foreign films in a festive setting. You can order pizza to be delivered here, or simply buy snacks, beer and soft drinks at the bar. And don't be choosy about what film is showing on the night you attend. It's the entire experience of watching a film under a sparkling Corfiot sky while sipping a cold Mythos beer that is so special – even if it is a B-movie that you'd never dream of watching back home.

From mid-Sept–May, Corfiot movie-goers repair to the indoor **Winter Cinema Orfeas** nearby on Yerásimou Aspióti. When the film finishes at about 11pm, things should just be getting under way at the **Jazz Rock Club** next door (tel: 26610 40640), one of Kérkyra's most pleasant and sophisticated nightspots, with live acts – often touring from the mainland or the rest of Europe – several nights weekly. Only drinks are available, and the summer garden at the back no longer operates, but the owner is contemplating reviving it so it's worth having a look after screenings at the Cinema Phoenix.

Above: stringing garlic

15. WESTERN BEACHES AND SPORT *(see map, p33)*

This hire car itinerary takes you on a strictly hedonistic tour of some of the west coast's beautiful beaches. You could take time out for a ride at the Rópa Valley Stables or a round of golf at the Corfu Golf Club.

To the starting point: if you want to play golf (choose 9 holes if you want time on the beach too), call the Corfu Golf Club (tel: 26610 94220) well in advance to reserve your tee time and club hire; the same applies to the horse riding (tel: 26610 94776/94220). Follow the same directions as for Itinerary 11 (see page 52), until you get just beyond the village of Kokkíni. Take bathing gear for the beach and sun protection for any of the day's activities.

Just beyond Kokkíni, following signs for the Louis Grand Hotel, turn left off the main road down to **Glyfádha Beach**. This is a long, long stretch of developed, but not ruined beachfront, dramatically situated and isolated by sheer vertical cliffs that plunge to the sea – and there is real surf here when the offshore wind is blowing hard. Watersports galore, sunbeds and umbrellas are on offer on the beach, and the crowd is fun-loving and young. There's an enormous car park at the foot of the cliffs. If you find that you like Glyfádha enough to return sometime for a longer stay, there are apartments and time-shared condominiums at **Menigos Beach Resort** (Glyfádha/Pélekas, Corfu, 49100 Greece; tel: 26610 95074, fax 26610 94933; e-mail: xenia_LTD@hotmail.com), an attractive place to stay, right on the beach; contact them well in advance of your visit. Have lunch at the **Agnes Restaurant** (tel: 26610 94231) halfway down the beach, where Agnes cooks simple Greek fare in her small kitchen.

Above: Glyfádha beach
Right: lunch at Agnes Restaurant

A Scenic Golfing Challenge

After a swim, retrace your route uphill to the Kokkíni/Érmones road, turn left and after 1km (½ mile), you will come to the **Corfu Golf Club** (near Érmones; tel/fax: 26610 94220), located in Corfu's idyllic and fertile Rópa Valley. Designed by Swiss-based course architect Donald Harradine, the 18-hole, Par 72-SSS 72 course blends the challenges and beauties of the valley's natural terrain with man-made hazards. It provides 'a good test, but a fair test', according to Course Manager and Head (PGA) Golf Pro, Jonathan Hunt, a native of Staffordshire in the UK, but a permanent resident of Corfu since 1991 (and perhaps the most photographed man – driver in hand – on the island). Featuring lakes, streams and copses of indigenous trees, the picturesque greens are among the Mediterranean's best kept secrets, but the Corfu Golf Club has many visiting players who come back time and again for the scenery, the quirky challenge of golfing in Greece, and the sheer pleasure of the laid-back atmosphere in the impressive clubhouse. Golfers and their families will all enjoy the facilities here. There's the inevitable pro shop with bags and clubs for hire (and, of course, club shirts for sale), a bar and lounge with satellite television and pool tables, a clubhouse restaurant which is open all day for snacks as well as full meals, and there are showers and changing facilities where you can freshen up after the game.

Mr Hunt offers various lessons ranging from 30- to 60-minute sessions and 9-holes tuition (for individuals or groups of two or three golfers) to courses of six lessons. Green fees (subject to change) start at €47 for 18 holes, but if you want to play every day for a week, this goes down to €30 a day, with an eighth day thrown in for free. Hiring golf cars, trolleys, clubs and driving range balls is extra, and you must book in advance.

Rópa Valley on Horseback

Adjacent to the golf clubhouse are the **Rópa Valley Stables** (tel: 26610 94776/94220; spring to autumn, rides at 9.30am and 3pm; fee includes refreshments) managed by Julie Haywood, who came originally from Nottingham. Noel Kirby, from Limerick, is Rópa's trek leader and wrangler; formerly an Irish folk musician of some renown, he is also a man who has a deep and obvious love of horses, and he leads treks, for individuals or small groups, through the Rópa Valley countryside. In spring, especially, these rides are a delight, not only for equestrians, but also for anyone interested in flora or butterflies.

Each of the two regularly scheduled daily rides lasts for two hours and includes refreshments at a nearby taverna, and knowledgeable Mr Kirby gives a running commentary on Corfiot flora and fauna. On horseback, riding through the silent fields, you will feel you have ridden back at least a millennium in time, and it's a fine way indeed to experience this lovely part of Corfu.

Left: eating on the hoof
Top Right: Nafiska taverna. **Right:** the Kaiser's Bridge

Sunset over Pélekas

Beyond the golf course and riding stables, you can continue for 1km (just over ½ mile) to the **Érmones Beach** community. Here, you can take a small boat to Apelístra and Andipsós beachlets, accessible only by sea. There's a scuba diving school below the vast Sunmarotel complex (and it's fun to ride the *téléferique* up to the hotel, with its grand view and huge swimming pool). The no-frills Nafsika taverna, on a hill overlooking the beach, is a good spot for coffee or cold drinks.

Below **Pélekas**, on your way back to Kérkyra, you will pass signs for Pélekas beach and Yialiskári beach: the first large and fairly developed, the latter smaller and more dramatically situated, with a quiet snack bar on the beach. If you happen to be near Pélekas around sunset on a summer's evening, take to the heights above the village, and seek out Kaiser Wilhelm II's well-signed little tower-with-a-telescope. Popularly known as 'the Kaiser's Throne', this is one of the best (and, in high season, one of the busiest) places on the west coast from which to view the sunset.

16. THE WILD, WOOLLY EAST *(see map, p49)*

This itinerary takes you down the heavily developed east coast, through the busy seaside resort of Benítses, then inland and up into the hills to pastoral Hlomós, dipping down finally to wild and woolly Kávos.

To the starting point: pick up a hire car and leave Kérkyra via the main Airport/Lefkími road.

Bear left following signs for Benítses and Lefkími, and 6km (4 miles) out of town, on your left, you will see the little peninsula of Kanóni, the monastery and church of Panaghía Vlahernón, and Pondikoníssi *(see pages 35 and 37)*. Some 9km (5½ miles) after leaving Kérkyra, you will see on your left

northeast coast (Mon, Wed, Fri, approximately 10.30am–5pm). For an extremely reasonable fare, exclusive of snacks and meals ashore (which are also reasonably priced), you will have an experience of the island that is not possible via wheeled transport: the coves and tiny, pristine beaches called at by the *Vivi* are only accessible from the sea. Don't forget to take along sunhats and sunglasses, sunblock, beach towels, bathing costumes, swimming shoes (for protection against sea urchins) and pre-frozen bottles of drinking water.

Durrell's Swimming Place

Iakis picks up his passengers at two or three prearranged rendezvous points, then heads lazily up the northeast coast, stopping at tiny coves en route to show you marine caves and the tiny seaside **Chapel of Ághios Arsénios**, perched atop picturesquely buckling sedimentary strata. The sea here is azure and pristine, and the rocky coast is just incredibly beautiful. It was at Ághios Arsénios that novelist Lawrence Durrell and his wife once dropped cherries into the clear waters. This was, with good reason, the British author's favourite bathing spot on Corfu.

At **Kouloúra**, Iakis will usually break out the ouzo and fruit juice for one and all. On the coast here, too, your captain will point out the villas that belong to the rich and famous – the late Gianni Agnelli (of Fiat) had a residence here, as Jacob Rothschild still does. The straits between Corfu and Albania now narrow dramatically and the *Vivi* is frequently passed by Greek Coast Guard vessels patrolling the waterway.

Further north, you drop anchor at **Ariás Beach**, deserted except for the day-visiting pleasure craft and their passengers, and have a swim in the transparent waters. If you have a snorkel and mask, it's fun to explore underwater here, but watch out for the occasional sea urchin.

After your swim, Iakis will head back to **Ághios Stéfanos Sinión**, and stop an hour or so here while you have lunch and sunbathe on the beach. He usually drops you at the **Taverna Galini** (tel: 26630 81492), where the best choices on the menu are fresh fish or a fresh pork *brizola* (chop), drenched in oregano and lemon juice. Good local wines are available here, too.

After another half hour or so at sea, the *Vivi* again anchors at **Kalámi Bay**. Lawrence Durrell once made his home here in the **White House**, which today comprises rooms for rent upstairs and a good restaurant downstairs. Peek inside at photos and framed clippings about Kalámi's most famous former resident, and have a cup of Greek coffee or an ice cream on the café terrace overlooking the sea. From here, at about 5pm, it's back to your point of embarkation.

Above: the Chapel of Ághios Arsénios
Top Right: the *Vivi* moors. **Right:** taking a look over the side

It is possible to take other trips on the *Vivi*. On Tuesday, Thursday and Saturday Iakis takes passengers south, again from Barbáti or Glyfáda, to Kérkyra for shopping and sightseeing, and to Vídhos islet for a swim. On Sunday, in season, there's a special 'Fresh Fish Barbecue Cruise' and, twice a week, romantic 'Sunset Cruises' to secluded beach tavernas.

Underwater Corfu

Another way of experiencing Corfu's fabulous east coast is underwater with a scuba tank. Arrange a scuba diving excursion in advance with Mr Christos Mourikis of the **Professional Diving Center** (2 Ioánnou Gardhikióti Street, Gouviá Marina; tel: 26610 91955; mobile: 6944317646; fax: 26610 26909), located within the Marina at Gouviá. Mr Mourikis offers dives and diving courses of all kinds – and is not averse to taking the occasional snorkeller out on his boat as well. If you're not certified as a scuba diver and want just a splash of underwater Corfu, you may opt for the centre's 'one-day, one-dive' option, accompanied by a professional scuba diving instructor. A wide selection of other courses is also available here. At whatever level of proficiency you choose to enter Corfu's underwater world you will take away indelible memories of this island.

If you're interested in chartering a yacht, next door to the Professional Diving Center, you will also find **OCC Yachting** (PO Box 171; Kérkyra, Corfu, 49100 Greece; tel/fax: 26610 99262; e-mail: info@occyachting.com; website: www.occyachting.com). Owned by Corfiot/Dutch Mr Menno Broodwinner, OCC Yachting maintains some 25 yachts here, ranging from 8 to 13m (27 to 42ft), available bare boat/self sail or as members of a flotilla – and the fees are very reasonable for Corfu.

Books and Music

Lykoudhis Bookstore
65 Voulgáreos Street
Kérkyra
Tel: 26610 39845
This bookshop and stationer's has served the public for 40 years. Likoudis also stocks a wide selection of foreign language books and maps on Corfu.

Mouses (Muses) Record Shop
9 and 22 Mihaïl Theotóki Street
Kérkyra
Tel: 26610 30708/37954/36994
A floor-to-ceiling, wall-to-wall trove of Greek and imported CDs, and a great place to procure 'audible memories' of your Corfiot sojourn. Ask owner Takis Alexandrou for help: his shop is about the best in Greece for breadth of selection and friendly service.

Food and Drink

Andriotis Traditional Patisserie & Cake Shop
1 Maniarízi keh Arlióti Street (Kandoúni Bízi)
Kérkyra
Tel: 26610 38045/38013
This is a no-frills, family-run and superlative Greek sweet shop with variations on Corfu's sugary kumquat theme and traditional Greek confections of all sorts.

Kava Païpeti
7 Maniarízi keh Arlióti Street (Kandoúni Bízi)
Kérkyra
Tel: 26610 30778/26620
There is kumquat liqueur or whole kumquats in syrup in quantity here, but this *kava* (wine cellar/off license) is really noted for its phenomenal selection of fine wine – Greek (from some 400 wineries), French and Italian.

Starenio
51 Guílford Street
Kérkyra
Tel: 26610 47370
Friendly Mr Nikos Kondopoulos runs this emporium of baked goods, sweets and traditional Greek foodstuffs – a treat for the eye, nose and taste buds. There's *mandoláto* (almond nougat), *mandóles* (burnt sugared almonds), Corfiot biscuits of all sorts, a cornucopia of breads (garlic, olive, olive oil, corn, honey and sunflower seed, honey and walnut) and traditional Greek pastries.

Jewellery

Gemini
50 Paleológou Street
Kérkyra
Tel: 26610 31107
Corfiot sculptor-jeweller Mr Nikos Michalopoulos's shop is tucked away near the Commercial Bank, but it's worth seeking out. His intensely sculptural and abstract jewellery, primarily in silver but also in gold, is inspired by the underwater world of the Ionian Sea.

Ilias Lalaounis
35 Kapodhistríou Street
Kérkyra
Tel: 26610 36258
Greece's 'ambassadors of gold', Mr Ilias Lalaounis and his family, have put the country firmly on the international map as far as gold jewellery is concerned. With many locations throughout Greece and the world, Lalaounis's designs in gold, semi-precious and precious stones are always fresh, creative, impeccably finished and, unlike much Greek gold, light enough to wear comfortably.

Mag
36 Nikifórou Theotóki Street

Kérkyra
Tel: 26610 43580)

Mr and Mrs Michael and Elsi Agistriotis's Mag (a Belgian-Greek jewellery concern with other shops on Corfu, in mainland Greece and Antwerp) features a wealth of sophisticated gold and silver jewellery. Especially beautiful are Mag's interpretations of Greek Byzantine pieces in gold and precious stones, created by hand using ancient skills.

Miscellaneous
English Imports
1st Párodhos Mitropolíti Methodhíou Street, off San Rocco Square
Kérkyra
Tel: 26610 47692

One of the permanent foreign community's favourite haunts, this little shop carries UK chain store goods, linens, clothing, gift items, periodicals and books. (Look for author Hilary Whitton-Païpeti's books, especially.) Run by Susan, Jane and Diana, the store features a bulletin board listing a treasure trove of local information.

Kannabishop
46 Kaloherétou Street, by Ághios Spyrídhon Church
Kérkyra
Tel: 26610 31114

This quirky little store is dedicated to the glories of hemp, aka the marijuana plant. Find hemp clothing, shoes, accessories, stationery and cosmetics here and, as Kannabishop's motto goes: 'Be friend with nature, be part of the solution' *(sic)*.

Mandala
16 Sevastianoú Street
Kérkyra
Tel: 26610 32705

Mr Friderikos Avgerinos visits India and Nepal each year, off season, and buys stock for his distinctive shop – textiles, statuary, clothing, jewellery and accessories. It's a lovely little oasis just off the Listón.

Tobacconists/Newsagents/ Photographic Supplies
Kiosk
11 Kapodhistríou Street and 9 Velissaríou Street
Kérkyra
Tel: 26610 42760

Operated by the Grammenos family, these newsagents and tobacconists have a staggering array of newspapers and periodicals especially foreign-language, plus cigarettes and cigars, including Havanas.

Photo Fast Liston
11/A Kapodhistríou Street, behind the Listón
Kérkyra
Tel: 26610 21629

Photographer Mr Yiannis Vlachos and his colleagues will get your prints back to you in under an hour, but this little shop also carries camera supplies and film in a convenient location.

Photo Tabac Ghitsis
52 Nikifórou Theotóki Street
Kérkyra
Tel: 26610 32005

This chock-a-block hole-in-the-wall has everything you could need in terms of tobacco, Cuban cigars, collectible toys, camera equipment, batteries, portable electronic equipment, etc. Open 7.30am till midnight in summer.

For those looking for a little slice of home-from-home shopping – though be aware that clothing stocks are tweaked to fit local tastes – the following listings in Kérkyra may be of interest: **The Body Shop**, tel: 26610 26539, 13 Platía Iróön Kypriakoú Agóna; **Marks & Spencer**, tel: 26610 41360, 15–17 Yeorghíou Theotóki Street; and **Benetton**, tel: 26610 23900, 9 Platía Iróön Kypriakoú Agóna.

EATING OUT

The Food of Corfu
by Diana Farr Louis

Corfiot cooking is quintessentially Mediterranean: laced with sweet virgin olive oil balanced with the acidity of tomatoes and lemon juice, heady with garlic and reliant on herbs like basil, mint and parsley for taste. Occasionally the Corfiots – alone among the Ionian islanders – spice their food with paprika, both hot and sweet, a habit whose origin is still debated.

Unlike most of the rest of Greece, Corfu was never occupied by the Ottoman Turks. Instead, its cuisine, like its architecture, reflects the lengthy presence of the Venetians and, to a lesser extent, the British. On

Left: kumquats come in many guises

many menus you'll find dishes with deceptively Italian-sounding names, like *bourdhétto* (fish sauced with tomato spiked with cayenne), *sofríto* (veal simmered with parsley, garlic and vinegar) and *pastitsádha* (a rich concoction of veal or cockerel stewed with onion and garlic, wine, tomato and cinnamon and served with thick macaroni), along with English puddings and *tsitsibýra* (ginger beer), served in some Listón cafés to go with a cricket game on the Spianádha.

In the old days, *bourdhétto*, *pastitsádha* and *sofríto* were party dishes prepared for a name day or special occasion by town folk. The country people were alarmingly poor and subsisted on a diet of wild greens, olive oil and bread, with an occasional rabbit or partridge. Even the more affluent ate far more sparingly than we do today. Surprisingly, many still hanker for 'poor people's food' – look for *tsigarélli* (sautéed greens with a touch of paprika).

The Corfiots prefer fruit for dessert and eat their sweets after the afternoon siesta or, at the risk of ruining their appetite, before dinner. These could be oriental pastries or ice cream, but the island is famous for its aromatic wild strawberries in late spring, *sykomaïdha* (fig bread) laced with grape must, brandy, ouzo and orange peel in autumn, and kumquats, fresh, glacéed or made into a bright orange liqueur that is unexpectedly delicious when added to fruit salads.

Restaurants

Eating out on Corfu can be hit or miss. All the restaurants have been personally, repeatedly and happily tested by Insight authors. The price guide is as follows: € = inexpensive; €€ = moderate; and €€€ = expensive.

Ághios Ioánnis
Spyros and Vasilis: Cuisine Française
Tel: 26610 52552/52438
On a hill in peaceful, rolling fields, near Tríklino and adjacent to Aqualand, is a surprise find: a fine French-with-a-Hellenic-twist restaurant. Start with pan-sautéed frogs' legs or mussels in cream. Follow that with the *Filet Spyros*, and finish with a *Soufflé au Grand Marnier*, a cheese platter or *Crêpes Suzettes* (if you want soufflés and crêpes, say so when you reserve a table). Extensive wine list. Open all year; veranda tables in summer. €€

Ághios Matthéos
Alonaki Bay Taverna
Tel: 26610 76118/9/75872
One of the locals' best-kept secrets until now, this little taverna, run by the Varagoulis family, shelters under windswept and stunted trees above little Alonáki Bay. It serves up fresh fish, eels, octopus and tiny Lake Korissíon shrimp, and you'll never want to leave, but there are rooms to rent here. €

Agní

Agni Taverna

Tel: 26630 91142

The entire family gets into the act at this delectable beachfront restaurant, including English son-in-law, Nathan, and Theodore who brings in the daily catch. Try the king prawn *saganáki* or garlic prawns; there's Stilton and port to round off the meal. €€

Toula

Tel: 26630 91350

Famous for its professional demeanour, nice line in hot *mezédhes* and the house special *garídhes* (shrimps) Toula – grilled prawns with spicy mixed-rice pilaff. Excellent bulk white wine and house desserts to round it off; open for lunch and supper much of the year. €€

Ághios Stéfanos Sinión

Eucalyptus (Evkalyptos)

North end of bay

Tel: 26630 82007

Housed in an old stone building, but with outdoor tables, weather permitting, this is probably the best, and best-value taverna in what can be a pretentious resort. They present a good mix of grilled seafood or meat, and Corfiot casserole dishes with innovative flavourings. Open May–Oct; best at lunch, as they tend to run out of food fairly early in the evening by Greek standards. €€

Avláki Bay

Cavo Barbaro (Fotis)

Tel: 26630 81905

An unusually good beach taverna, easy of access while touring the north coast, with welcoming service. A few pre-cooked dishes at lunch, like 'risotto' and *soudzoukákia*, more grills after dark, plus homemade *glyká koutalioú* (candied fruit). Seating on the lawn, and plenty of parking. The only thing 'barbarous' here can be the wind, as there's no shelter; check direction and strength before heading downhill. €

Gastoúri

Bella Vista

Tel: 26610 56232

Hilltop restaurant that lives up to its name, taking in a view extending from the Achilleion Palace to Epirus across the straits. Best for *mayireftá* meat dishes and grills,

and a good choice if you've just visited the palace. Open Easter–Oct Tues–Sun; weekends only off-season. €€

Káto Korakiána

Etrusco

Tel: 26610 93342

Top-calibre nouvelle Italian cooking purveyed by the Bottrini family – father, son and spouses – served since 1992 at a carefully restored country manor. Specialities like home-made cured meat, *timpano parpadellas* (pasta with duck and truffles) and a 200-label wine list don't come cheaply though – budget a minimum €30 each before drink. Open Apr–Oct, supper only; reservations essential. €€€

Kérkyra Town

Aegli Restaurant

23 Kapodhistríou Street

Tel: 26610 31949

Promoted as the oldest traditional restaurant in Kérkyra (established in 1812), the Aegli is linen-napkin respectable and open all day. From the Corfiot specialities, try the veal or cockerel *pastitsáda*, veal *sofríto*, or *kléftiko* (lamb and onion fricassee). €€

Alekos' Beach

Bánio tou Alékou quay, below Faliráki complex

(no phone)

Alekos' limited menu revolves around grills, seafood and salads, but it's very reasonably priced for the stunning location – right by the waterside, with views of the illuminated Paleó Froúrio by night. Open in summer only. €

Left: a meeting of like minds
Right: service at the Rex

Arpi

10 Yiotopoúlou Street, off the Spianadha
Tel: 26610 27715

Charming Mr Spyros Kasimis, of Othoní islet, makes this place swing, putting his hand to everything. The food is traditional – but with flair. Try excellent starters such as hard cheese with pesto, and *skordaliá* (garlic and potato puree), and move on to spaghetti with mussels, the grilled salmon filet, or one of Spiros's daily specials. €

Del Sole Ristorante

17 Guílford Street, Pórta Remoúnda
Tel: 26610 32411

The Corfiot Metallinou family owns and operates this superb Italian restaurant, specialising in homemade fresh pastas. Try penne with tomato sauce and basil, spaghetti pesto, macaroni with gorgonzola, the roca and Parmesan salad, prosciutto croquettes – and leave room for the house cheesecake or *panna cotta*. Supper all year, lunch also May–Oct €€

Hryssomallis (alias **Babis**)

6 Nikifórou Theotókou
Tel: 26610 30342

The sign says a *zythopsitopolío* ('beer-hall–grill'), but it's also one of the last surviving traditional oven-food places in the old town: stews, *hórta*, *moussakás*, lamb offal, and so forth, all washed down with smooth but potent red wine. From the outside tables on the pedestrian street you can just see the Listón, while Venetian housefronts tower overhead; a typical bill won't run to more than €10–13 each. It's been around since 1839, and in the Statiris family since the 1950s; the Durrells ate here regularly during their 1930s stay on Corfu. €

La Cucina

15 Guílford Street, Pórta Remoúnda
Tel: 26610 45029

Another great Italian bistro on Guílford Street. Again, homemade pasta is the star, and there are some spectacular combinations on the menu: linguine with butterfly prawns, rocket, parsley, spring onions and a creamy *wasabi* sauce, or a pan-seared filet, and tortelloni with prosciutto. Feb–Nov, supper only. €€

La Famiglia

30 Maniarízi keh Arlióti Street (Kandoúni Bízi)
Tel: 26610 30270

Mr and Mrs Sandro and Maryo Campogiani run the town's most-popular mini-bistro, where pasta dishes featuring mature and baby clams *(vongole)*, an array of Italian antipasti and fresh quiches – plus puddings to die for – make reservations a must. €€

Mezedhakia

38–40 Ethnikís Antistáseos Street, New Port District
Tel: 26610 24931

Mezedhákia means 'little starters' in Greek, and this establishment serves up some 80 spectacular little appetisers, including peppers stuffed with cheese and courgette croquettes. Choosing from the vast array will be your dilemma. €

Mouraghia

15 Arseníou
Tel: 26610 33815

A good mix of seafood (with fresh and frozen items clearly indicated) and Corfiot *mayireftá* like *sofríto* and *pastitsádha* at this all-year *ouzerí* popular with families and students. Inexpensive for any island, let alone Corfu's old town, and great sea views in the bargain. €

O Yiannis

43 Aghíon Iásonos and Sosipatroú Street, Anemómylos Quarter
Tel: 26610 31066

Open since the late 1970s, this is a grand old taverna where you troop off to the kitchen to view the contents of some 15–20 cooking pots. The veal (either in lemon or oregano sauce), *stifádo* (stew), and *gávros* (anchovies, in tomato and onion) are all good choices. €€

Rex Restaurant

66 Kapodhistríou Street
Tel: 26610 39649

Since 1932, the Rex has been serving Corfiot specialities with flair. Try their *arní stámnas* (lamb simmered in a ceramic crock), or fish *bourdhétto*. End with a baked apple or *ravaní*, a Greek cake drenched in syrup. The service is impeccable all day long. €€

Tenedhos

1st Párodhos Solomoú, Spiliá district
Tel: 26610 36277

Despite all the silly stickers and brandished endorsements from guidebooks, this is actually an excellent choice for lunch or supper on the way to or from the Néo Froúrio looming overhead. The fare is given a French twist, with ample seafood choices, vegetarian *mezédhes* and Lefkími bulk wine. Locals go especially for the *kandádhes* in the evening, accompanied by acoustic (non-amplified guitar). Usually closed on Monday. €€

The Five Sisters/Pende Adherfes
151 Xen Stratigou Street
Tel: 26610 38263
Just off the port, this taverna caters mainly for locals and is run by the five Avgerinou sisters – Spyridoula, Eleftheria, Chryssoula, Sophia and Georgia. It is usually packed with diners tucking into enormous portions of charcoal-grilled lamb, beef, chicken, pork and sausage. Order a Greek salad, fries and barrel wine to go with the meat. €

Venetian Well
Platía Kremastí, northwest of the cathedral, Campiello district
Tel: 26610 44761
Tucked away through an arch, with outdoor tables around the namesake well, is arguably the town's most innovative – and expensive – cooking, generic Aegean with *nouvelle* twists. The interior, following a 2001 overhaul, eclectically draws on several oriental traditions. Recipes change yearly, depending on the proprietor's winter travels and inspiration, but in past seasons have encompassed duck breast with dried fruit, wholegrain rice *dolmádhes*, or pork chop with sun-dried tomatoes and peppers. An expensive wine list pushes this into the splurge category, but with the enchanted setting, there's no better place in town to fall in love with Corfu – or your dining companion. Mar–Oct, supper only. €€€

Lefkími
Maria
Riverbank, south quay
Tel: 26620 22150
Ideal for an inexpensive but tasty lunch of *mayireftá* (baked pork chops, baked fish, green beans, good bulk wine) while touring the far south; tables are under the trees overlooking the river. Maria herself, a traditionally dressed granny, is a never-ending fount of risqué anecdotes; crash course in baroquely elaborate Greek swearing free with your meal. €

Nissáki
Mitsos
Tel: 26630 91240
On the little rock-outcrop 'islet' *(nissáki)*, this ordinary-looking beachside taverna stands out for cheerful service from two partners. There's a high turnover which ensures that the fare, which includes fried local fish and well-executed *sofríto*, is always fresh. Open Apr–Oct, lunch and dinner . €

Paleá Períthia
Foros
Just off the central plaza
Tel: 26630 98373
This all-but-abandoned, perfectly preserved stone village on the north slopes of Mt Pandokrátor has two tavernas. This is the more down-to-earth, a little taverna-*ouzerí* specialising in its own cheese, one cooked dish per day, a few *píttas* (turnovers) and a choice

of grills. The food's perhaps not the best in the interior, but it's a supremely atmospheric setting with civil service. €

Paxí
Alexandhros
Lákka
Tel: 26620 30045
Considered the most authentic and reassuringly, hygienic *nisiótiko* cooking in this resort, with the most atmospheric setting – on the Platía Edward Kennedy (so named for his visit). The menu features own-produced grilled meat or chicken, specialities like *sofríto* and mushroom pie, plus a few seafood dishes, though the barrel wine should be avoided. €€

Right: three members of The Five Sisters taverna

14 Kapodhistríou Street
Tel: 26610 33883
Located right on the Spianádha, this is the place to go for billiards, with drinks. A little rough-and-ready in terms of clientele – but it's air conditioned!

Aperito
14 Ethnikís Antistásseos Street, New Port
Tel: 26610 40487
Ioannis Ionas's popular bar catering for the teens to thirties crowd, serves cold drinks, cocktails and coffees – and you can hear yourself think here. Open Mon–Fri 9pm–3.30am; later on Sat and Sun.

Apokalypsis
Ethnikís Andistásseos Street, in the Commercial Centre
Tel: 26610 40345
Now entering its third decade of life – a Methusaleh by Greek club standards – this giant disco with its mock-archaeological facade at the centre of the Evthía strip intersperses theme nights with mainstream music. Traditionally operated only Easter–Sept, but a new bar-restaurant inside, which opened in 2002, could extend its season.

Café Grec
5 Kapodhistríou Street
Tel: 26610 36645
Located just behind the Listón, and open all day (until 1am) for Portioli coffees, drinks and, eventually, cocktails, this is a well-loved little see-and-be-seen venue.

Café On Line
28 Kapodhistríou Street
Tel: 26610 46226
e-mail: cafe_online1@yahoo.com
website: www.corfu-net.gr/online
This buzzing internet café (with other locations in Moraïtika and Kassiópi) is a gathering place for Corfu's computer-literate of all nationalities. This place is made what it is by owners Kostas and Spyros's friendly multilingual hospitality (and Eleni's coffee). There's also a hot evening-into-night chess game here daily, plus outstanding *frappés* (iced coffee) and ice-cream. Open 10am–1am in high season.

Cavalieri Hotel Roof Garden
Cavalieri Hotel, 4 Kapodhistríou Street
Tel: 26610 39041/39336
One of the most romantic (and comprehensive) vantage points in the city, this roof garden overlooks the Spianádha, the Old Fortress and Garítsa Bay. The Cavalieri serves light meals, ice-cream, drinks and cocktails – with a lovely view. Open May–Oct, 6.30pm–4am,

Coca
30 Ethnikís Antistasséos Street, New Port
Tel: 26610 34477
Open from midnight on, this low-ceilinged, wood-and-stone dance club's been going strong for 25 years. A drinks-and-music only venue, the outdoor bar attracts a slightly more mature crowd. Often hosts foreign DJs in high season. Open daily Apr–Oct, weekend only otherwise.

Ekati
Alykés Potamoú Street
Tel: 26610 45920/27000
This upmarket, modern Greek-style nightclub on the outskirts of Kérkyra features excellent live *bouzoúki* bands with vocalists, and caters for a very well-heeled, over-30 Greek crowd. Cocktails and bottles of whisky, dinners and snacks are all expensive. It's really only worth going very late at weekends (around 1–5am) and in winter it's only open on Friday and Saturday anyway. It's also a good idea to phone ahead for reservations.

Hippodrome
52 Ethnikís Antistásseos Street, New Port
Tel: 26610 35385
A huge, well-established disco-with-swimming-pool, the Hippodrome opens at midnight, but really doesn't start cooking till hours later. Musical format progresses from ambient to House. In winter, its clientele is made up mostly of Corfiot teenagers, while in summer, it becomes the popular wee-hours haunt of Italian and English visitors.

Hook
5 Kapodhistríou Street
Tel: 26610 47131
An elegant little bar that spills out into the Spianádha, next door to the Cavalieri Hotel, the Hook features rock music, a full bar and Carlsberg on tap. Also open in the morning for coffee.

Jazz Rock Club
3 Yerásimou Aspióti Street, next to Cinema Orfeas
Tel: 26610 40640
Indoor winter (Oct–May) premises feature live jazz dates by reputable Greek and

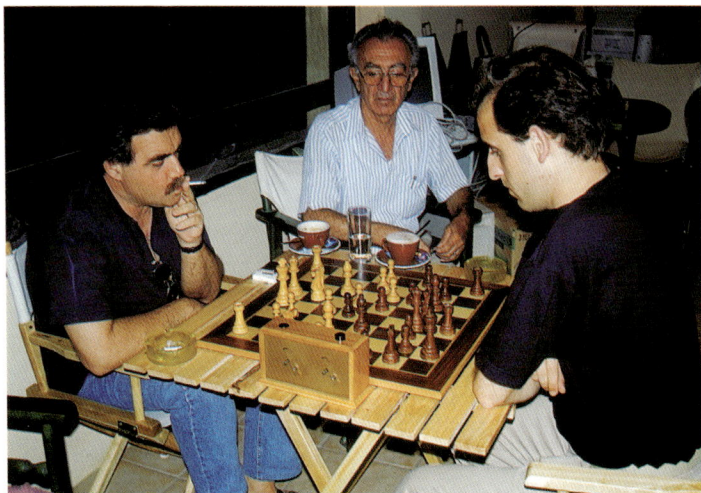

foreign acts such as Mode Plagal – the only such venue on the island; hot and cold drinks accompany the sounds. The much-loved summer garden-bistro out back ceased operating in 2001, but may reopen in future seasons – check.

Magnet
102 Kapodhistríou Street
Tel: 26610 45295
At the noisy (duelling rock music at adjacent bars) end of the Listón is Magnet, a popular if pricy café/bar that's packed soon after the sun goes down. Order drinks and cocktails here after dinner and before moving on to the Evthía dance club district.

NetOikos Café
14 Kaloherétou Street
Tel: 26610 47481
website: www.netoikos.gr/
This is a swinging, if smoke-filled spot to meet others in cyberspace. Cool decor and a nice, full bar. Open Mon–Fri 9am–1am, Sat 11am–1am, Sun 11am–11pm; like its rival, Café On Line, it charges rates of €6–7 per hour.

Sax
68 Ethnikís Antistásseos Street, New Port
Tel: 26610 21757
This club is known as the one to head for after all the rest have closed down. Small, often airless bar area, shady courtyard for 'chilling out'. Guest DJs in summer. Open Mon–Fri, midnight–3am, much later at weekends.

Show
42 Ethnikís Antistasséos Street, New Port
Tel: 26610 80780
This club, which opened in the late 1990s, has been designed to have the appearance of an archaeological site on the Nile – wild! It attracts a slightly more mature, slightly trendier crowd than many of the neighbouring venues. Next door, the management has opened Smooth, a convenient restaurant-cum-snack-bar for those who want a nice bite to eat before or after dancing and drinking. Open midnight until the wee hours, and busy at weekends; more Greek than foreign sounds.

Tzavarátika
Corfu By Night
Paleokastrítsa Highway (just north of Gouviá)
Tel: 26610 91733
Like the Ekati, Corfu By Night is an authentic Greek *skyládhiko* or roadhouse – that is to say it is devoted to heavily amplified *bouzoúki* ensembles and Greek vocalists; sometimes there are Greek dancers as well. It is in full swing only on Friday night and weekends from around 12.30–4am. This is the perfect place to see Corfiots enjoying their preferred genre of music. You should arrange for a taxi to pick you up after the show, and call in advance for programme information and reservations. Drinks, by the glass or full bottles, and food are pricy and there is also a cover charge.

Above: strategic moves at Café On Line

CALENDAR OF EVENTS

The Greek year is delightfully interspersed with ancient, Christian or patriotic holidays: Greek Orthodox Easter, the anniversary of a popular revolution or local victory, or the name day of a beloved saint. These name days, or saints' days – *yiortés* in Greek – are very important to Greeks, who barely note their own birthdays but entertain family and friends lavishly on the evening of their own saint's name day. Often, entire villages turn out – with parades, a street fair, and church services – to honour a saint whose church is pre-eminent in their town.

Four great annual processions are held to honour St Spyrídhon *(see page 16)*, and his name day, 12 December, is all but a pan-island holiday, since so many Corfiots bear the name Spiridon, Spiros or Spiridoula.

January

1 Ághios Vasílios (St Basil). Holiday gifts are exchanged and the *vassilópitta* – a cake with a coin baked in it for luck – is ritually cut.
6 Ta Fóta (Epiphany). National holiday. Blessing of the waters, to commemorate Christ's baptism, at the little port of Mandhráki, beneath the Old Fortress in Corfu/Kérkyra Town.

February

2 Ypapandí (Candlemas). The Presentation of Christ at the Temple. Festivities at the Church of Ypapandí in Komméno.

Variable date. Apókries. The three-week period preceding Greek Orthodox Lent is Greece's Carnival Season. Fancy dress parties, masked balls, parades with floats and marching bands, and peculiarly Corfiot variations on the Carnival theme.

March

8 Aghía Theodhóra (St Theodora). The saint's relics are carried in a procession around Kérkyra.
25 Greek Independence Day; also **Evangelismós (Annunciation)**. National holiday commemorating the beginning of the Greek Revolution against the Ottoman Turks in 1821.
Variable date. Katharí Dheftéra (Clean Monday). National holiday marking the first day of Lenten fasting, seven weeks before Easter. Kite-flying and picnics with special Lenten fare. Carnival parade at Perouládhes.

April

Variable date. Greek Orthodox Easter. Almost always in April.
Palm Sunday. Procession with St Spyrídhon's relics *(see page 16)* and marching bands through Kérkyra; feast of salt cod.
Megáli Evdhomádha (Holy Week). Many Greeks fast for this entire week, especially on Good Friday, which resembles a day of national mourning throughout the country.
Holy Tuesday. Choir recitals at the church of Ághios Spyrídhonos, the Church of Aghía Paraskeví and the Metropolitan Cathedral.
Holy Wednesday. Concert of hymns by the Municipal Choir at the Municipal Theatre.
Holy Thursday. Service of the Twelve Gospels is held at the Catholic Cathedral, in Platía Dhimarhíou.
Megáli Paraskeví (Good Friday). National holiday. Sombre rites surrounding the *Epitáfios* (Christ's Funeral Bier). Biers from many churches, accompanied by marching bands, process through Kérkyra.
Megálo Sávvato (Holy Saturday). Procession of St Spyrídhon's relics through Kérkyra *(see page 16)*; various services and traditional events. At midnight the Lenten fast is broken with red-dyed eggs, special lamb tripe soup and loaves baked in the shape of doves. Festivities, complete with fireworks and marching bands, are best viewed from the Spianádha.

Left: parading in Corfiot costume

Páskha (Greek Orthodox Easter).
National holiday. The most important day of
the Greek year is celebrated with feasting
and joyful recreation. Corfiot churches pro-
cess icons of the Resurrection.
Easter Monday. Processions with noisy and
dangerous fireworks.
Easter Tuesday. At 5pm, St Spyrídhon's
relics are returned to the Church of Ághios
Spyrídhonos.
Friday after Easter. *Zoödhóhos Pighí* (The
Font of Life) celebration at Paleokastrítsa.
Sunday after Easter. St Thomas. Proces-
sion and festivities at Epískepsi and Sidhári.

May

1 May Day/Labour Day. National holiday.
Workers' parades and excursions to the
countryside to gather flowers and greenery
for May wreaths.
21 SS Constantine and Helen. Also celebrating the union of Ionian Islands with
Greece.

June

**Variable date. Pendekostí (Pentecost/Whit
Sunday).** Celebrated seven weeks after
Easter with festivities throughout Corfu.
Aghíou Pnévmatos (Whit Monday).
National holiday.
12 Ághios Onoúfrios. Festivities at Pélekas.
29 SS Peter and Paul. Festivities at many
villages throughout Corfu; major festival at
Gaïos, Paxí.

July

2 Panaghía Vlahernón. Festivities at
Aharávi, Garítsa and Kamára and at Fondána
on Paxí.
12 St Spyrídhon. One of several days dedicated annually to the island's patron saint
(see page 16).
13 Aghía Marína. Festivities at Avliótes,
Benítses, Sparterá and in San Rocco Square,
Kérkyra.

August

1–6 Christ The Saviour. Six days of festivities at the Monastery of the Pandokrátor.
**6 Metamórfosi (Transfiguration of
Christ).** Festivities in the Campiello Quarter of Kérkyra and throughout Corfu.
10 Varkarola. Concert of *kandádhes*,

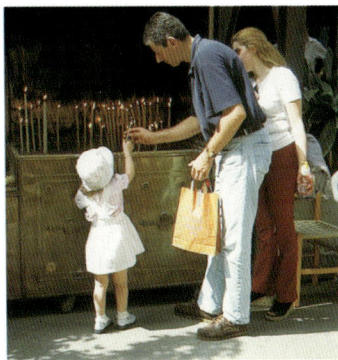

traditional Ionian Island songs, from water-
craft anchored in Garítsa Bay.
11 St Spyrídhon. Yet another of the days
dedicated to the memory of the saint. Procession in Corfu/Kérkyra Town; festivities
throughout the island.
**15 The Dormition/Assumption of The Vir-
gin Mary.** National holiday with festivities
the length and breadth of Corfu.

September

In September, the International Festival of
Classical Music is held on Paxí.

October

28 'Ohi' ('No') Day. National holiday commemorating Metaxas' standing up to Mus-
solini and the Italian invasion (with his
famous 'No!') in 1940.

November

**15 Start of the Fast of the Nativity ('Lit-
tle Lent').**
17 Polytechnion Day. School holiday and
early business closings. Commemorates the
sit-in and subsequent massacre at the Athens
Polytechnical School which led to the fall of
the 1970s junta.

December

6 Ághios Nikólaos (St Nicholas). Christmas
festivities the length and breadth of Corfu.
12 St Spyrídhon's Day. Local holiday. Two-
day festivities in Kérkyra. Festivities in Kav-
vadádes, Spartýlas, Kanáli, Vasilátika and
Velonádes.
25 Hristoúghema (Christmas).
26 Gathering of the Virgin's Entourage.
31 New Year's Eve.

Above Right: lighting a candle at Ághios Spyrídhonos

Practical Information

GETTING THERE

Unfortunately, there are currently no scheduled airline flights from anywhere (apart from internal flights from Athens) to Corfu, but in the brave new world of no-frills carriers, and with over 10,000 foreign residents on this island, this could very well change, with rumours abounding of easyJet inaugurating links with England in coming years. For the moment, you'll have to content yourself with a flight first to Athens, and then to Corfu (the only option for North Americans), or a seasonal direct charter flight from cities in the rest of Europe to Corfu. With careful planning and an eye to layover times, it's usually not necessary to spend a night in Athens en route unless you explicitly wish to.

From the UK, only British Airways, Olympic and easyJet fly direct to Athens, while from North America only Delta offers a non-stop service. Especially coming from North America, you will find that fares drop considerably if your flight includes a one-stop itinerary via Rome, Frankfurt or Zurich (these are the most common hubs). Additionally, recourse to internet travel sites such as www.expedia.com/co.uk, www.travelselect.com, www.cheapflights.co.uk or www.a2b.com should turn up a number of attractive options. Or try the airlines' own sites (except for Olympic, which does not allow on-line purchases); most offer a slight discount for booking on line, and with their e-tickets there's no chance for paper tickets to go astray in the post.

Most airports in Germany and Britain, as well as the Netherlands, Italy, Scandanavia, Switzerland, the Czech Republic and even Russia or Poland offer something weekly or more frequently between Easter and mid-October. It is almost always cheaper to use a direct charter package to the island than a scheduled fare, even if you don't use the basic accommodation included.

By Air from Greece

Greek domestic carriers Aegean Cronus and Olympic Airways between them fly several times daily from Athens and (far less often) Thessaloníki to Corfu. Financially strapped Olympic offers at most three bizarrely timed daily flights to the island all year from Athens; their two weekly flights from Thessaloníki also go fairly late at night. Aegean Cronus provides two far more user-friendly daily departures from Athens throughout the year. Flight time from Athens is just under an hour, and prices are fairly steep (typically €160 return in summer) for the distance involved, though you can occasionally find promotional fares of €130 or even €100. With the recent decrease in flight frequency, it is necessary to book at least two weeks in advance, even during spring or autumn.

Useful phone numbers and websites:

Ioannis Kapodhistrias Airport, Corfu, general info, tel: 26610 30180

Aegean Cronus, airport, tel: 26610 27100

Olympic Airways, Polylá 11, Kérkyra, tel: 26610 38694

Olympic Airways, airport, tel: 26610 37398

Olympic Airways, nationwide reduced-rate number: 801 1144444

Aegean Cronus, nationwide reduced-rate number: 801 1120000

www.olympic-airways.gr

www.aegeanair.com

By Road

The nearest Greek mainland port of call for Corfu is Igoumenítsa, which is served by regularly scheduled bus service from Athens and Thessaloníki. There are also car ferry connections to Corfu from Pátra, which is much more quickly accessible from Athens by train, bus or private car (3–4 hours depending on traffic).

KTEL (Intercity Bus Service): for information in Athens, tel: 210 512-9443; in Igoumenítsa, tel: 26650 22309; in Ioánnina, tel: 0651 26404; in Pátra, tel: 2610 222271.

Left: forward planning

By Sea

There's a wide variety of fairly consistent car ferry, catamaran and hydrofoil links between Corfu and Pátra, Igoumenítsa and (rarely) Saghiádha on the Greek mainland, as well as with Ancona, Bari, Brindisi, Trieste and Venice in Italy. Domestic ferries connect Corfu also with the nearby Dhiapóndia islets to the north and Paxí to the south. The main destination on Corfu is Kérkyra's New Port, but Lefkími in the south is also useful, especially for car-drivers approaching from Igoumenítsa.

In season, there are frequent (almost two-hourly) car-ferry services from Igoumenítsa to Kérkyra; crews are (unusually for Greece) courteous and efficient, and fares for a car and driver together run at about €22. The journey takes 1 hour 45 minutes, though you can trim this – and the fare – to about an hour and €13 by using the crossing to Lefkími which operates about six times daily. Hydrofoils (no cars carried) between Igoumenítsa and Kérkyra take half the time at roughly double the price.

For getting to the Dhiapóndia islets, there is a slow car ferry from Kérkyra (2–4 times weekly depending on season), though most people visit on the passenger-only caiques out of Sidhári or Ághios Stéfanos Avliotón (3–6 days weekly depending on demand).

Paxí is served by at least five slow weekly ferries year-round from Kérkyra; in season this rises to at least two daily, with an extra hydrofoil departure thrown in. In season, the Igoumenítsa-Paxí sea lane is also served by both sorts of craft, which may involve triangular routings out of Lefkími or Kérkyra.

	Avge Temp (C/F)	Avge Rainy Days
January	12/53	12
February	15/59	12
March	13/57	9
April	16/60	9
May	19/66	6
June	23/73	4
July	26/79	1
August	26/79	1
September	23/73	5
October	19/66	11
November	15/59	11
Dec	12/54	15

From Italy, at least one shipping company calls at Kérkyra's New Port every day except perhaps January and February. Fares vary widely depending on speed and comfort of craft and, of course, according to start-point (Bari/Brindisi are the shortest and cheapest, Venice/Trieste the most expensive). Most, though not all, departures are overnight; budget a minimum of €120 for two people in a cabin plus a small car, taxes included.

International ferry schedules tend to be quite reliable, though the most current information source are the various companies' websites. Printed domestic schedules (rarely) seen in Greece tend to be obsolete or fantastic (in the literal sense) the minute they're off the press; the only firm information on sailings is to be had by strolling down to the quayside ticket booths in person, or by contacting the following *limenarhía* or port authorities:

Kérkyra: tel: 26610 32655
Lefkími: tel: 26620 23277
Igoumenítsa: tel: 26650 22235
Pátra: tel: 2610 341002 or 341024
Paxí (Gaïos): tel: 26620 32259
Saghiádha (July–Aug): tel: 26640 51217

TRAVEL ESSENTIALS

When to Visit

Corfu is at its best in spring, from Greek Orthodox Easter to June, when the island is awash with flowers, and then again after the high season, in September and October.

Visas and Passports

European Union, Australian, New Zealand, Canadian, US and most other non-European Union visitors need only a valid passport to visit Corfu; non-EU visitors are stamped in and out upon arrival/departure, which affords them an informal, 90-day tourist 'visa'.

Customs

Duty-free restrictions no longer apply within the EU, though goods carried must be for personal use only (officials have their own guidelines for what may reasonably be considered for personal use), and spot checks for illegal drugs may still occur. Entering Greece from outside the EU you are allowed to bring with you, duty-free: 200 cigarettes or 50 cigars; 1 litre (35fl oz) of spirits or 2 litres (70fl oz) of wine; 50g (1¾ oz) of perfume; 250ml (8¾fl oz) of eau de cologne; one camera and film; one pair of binoculars; a portable musical instrument; a portable radio or tape recorder; a laptop; sports equipment, and, with a veterinarian's certificate, dogs and cats. When carrying medicines, be sure to bring along the corresponding physicians' prescriptions; non-prescription medicines containing codeine are not permitted. You may import an unlimited amount of foreign currency, but if you intend to leave with foreign currency units amounting to over US$1,000, you must declare this amount upon entering Greece. It is a severely punishable offence to remove antiquities of any size or value from Greece.

Clothing

The Corfiot summer lasts from June to September, though light rain falls at both ends of the season, and a showerproof coat comes in handy. In high season it can be very hot, humid and sticky, so the most comfortable clothing is lightweight and made of natural fabrics – and be sure to bring enough, because laundry and dry-cleaning services, except at the top hotels, are primitive and slow. Pack sturdy shoes with crêpe soles for walking, or hiking boots if you plan more strenuous treks; sandals and plastic water shoes for the beach (to protect against sea urchins); high-SFP sunblock; a sunhat; extra pairs of prescription spectacles; snorkelling gear and a beach towel if you want; and modest clothing for visiting churches and monasteries – at least one long-sleeved garment for both men and women, plus long trousers and an over-the-knee skirt/dress, according to gender.

GETTING ACQUAINTED

Geography

Kérkyra lies 39° 38' North and 19° 54' East. The island has an area of about 593sq km (230sq miles), with a population of around 110,000, of whom some 33,000 live in the capital (2001 census) and of which a staggering 10 percent are foreign-born. The pre-

fecture of Corfu, Paxí, Andípaxi, Othoní, Eríkoussa and Mathráki constitutes the third most densely populated prefecture in Greece.

Religion

Unlike the rest of Greece, which is almost solely Greek Orthodox, Corfu has a significant Roman Catholic population, mostly of Maltese origin, who have their own cathedral in the capital. There are also Anglican, Evangelical and Jewish communities and congregations, all with their own places of worship.

How Not To Offend

The Ionian islands are rather more conservative than many of the Greek islands further south. Very modest dress is required in order to enter most monasteries and churches on the island; toplessness is tolerated on some beaches but is not the general rule; and there is only one openly nudist beach in all of Corfu *(see Itinerary 11, Page 52)*. There is also a visible police presence throughout the island, and drunkenness and other public misbehaviour is not tolerated (except, arguably, in Kávos).

How to Stay Safe

The British Consul on Corfu hands out a travel advisory leaflet for visitors featuring

Above: alms box, Angelókastro

a simple checklist for a safe, happy visit:
1) Bring sufficient funds. 2) When hiring a
vehicle, boat or moped, check to be sure it's
road- or sea-worthy, has sufficient insurance,
comes with safety equipment. 3) Women
should not walk home alone at night, nor
accept lifts from strangers or casual acquain-
tances. 4) When visiting historic sites,
remember that these are the favoured haunts
of bag-snatchers and thieves. 5) Do not get
involved with drugs in Greece, full stop. 6)
Do not expect to find work easily. 7) Respect
Greece's customs regulations. 8) Respect
Greece's laws in general. 9) Too much sun
mixed with alcohol usually results in serious
health problems.

Money Matters
Currency

Since February 2002, the currency of Greece
– along with 11 other European countries –
has been the euro (*evró* in Greek), subdi-
vided into 100 cents *(leptá)*. After a less than
impressive start, the euro has been steadily
gaining ground against the pound sterling
and the US dollar; as of writing a dollar is
worth only about 90 euro-cents, and the
pound fetches well under €1.50. Euros come
as notes of 500, 200, 100, 50, 20, 10 and 5,
while coins come as 2 euros, 1 euro, and 50,
20, 10, 5, 2 and 1 cent(s). Notes are the same
across the euro-area, but coins are struck by
each member country and thus vary (but are
valid across the euro-area).

Credit Cards

Many credit cards – VISA preferred – are
accepted at upmarket hotels, restaurants (but
not *tavernes*) and shops, but cash is always
preferred on Corfu, and will often earn you
a discount on goods. Note: always carry
some small-denomination notes as taxi
drivers will not change anything above a
50-euro note.

Cash Machines

Almost all Corfiot bank branches – and there
are many – have ATMs, though they may not
always be in working order.

Tipping

Leaving a tip of 10–15 percent of the bill is
customary for sterling service.

GETTING AROUND

Taxis

Corfu has a well organised and reliable radio
taxi service, vastly superior to the one in
Athens. Drivers are apt to be more honest
than their Athenian counterparts, and lost
or forgotten property may actually be
returned. The Association of Corfu Radio-
taxi Owners issues a pamphlet which lists
fares to and from various destinations, as
these rates on Corfu are set, not measured by
meter. Ask for this pamphlet if you plan to
make frequent use of radio taxis. Within
Kérkyra town the standard urban rates –
posted on a laminated dashboard placard –
apply. There are taxi ranks at the new and old
ports, at the south end of the Spianádha and
on Platía San Rocco.
Radio Taxi, 24-Hour Service, tel: 26610
33811

Bus

There are two fleets of buses on Corfu: blue
urban buses, with a terminus in San Rocco
Square (tel: 26610 31595), which serve
Kérkyra and its suburbs; and green-and-
cream long-distance buses, with a terminus
on Avramíou Street (tel: 26610 30627/
39985/39862), which ply further afield and
serve the rest of the island. A copy of the
most recent bus schedule can be found in
any issue of *The Corfiot*, an English-
language monthly magazine that can be
picked up from any newsagent in the capital. Tickets for blue buses are sold at kiosks
on the square; for long-distance buses,
they're sold on board.

Car

You may call or fax ahead, or book on an
international website and have a hire car
waiting for you at the airport on Corfu. You
can arrange for one through your hotel but,
in high season, cars may not be available
unless booked in advance. It is worth paying
the higher rate for all-inclusive insurance
coverage.

Major international car-hire chains and
a few local one-offs worth contacting
include:
Avis: New Port, tel: 26610 24404, fax: 26610
26826, airport: 26610 42007, www.avis.com

Budget: 32 Polyhroníou Konstandá, tel: 26610 28282, fax: 26610 28489, airport: 26610 28208, www.drivebudget.com

Eurodollar: Old Port, tel: 26610 46748

Europcar: 32 Venizélou, tel: 26610 46931, fax: 26610 46934, airport: 26610 46440, www.europcar.com

Hertz: Tripouléïka district, tel: 26610 38388, airport: 26610 35547, fax: 26610 24477, www.hertz.com

National/Alamo: 38 Venizélou, tel: 26610 49651, fax: 26610 49653, www.national-car.com

InterEurope: tel: 26610 24000, airport: 26610 36689

Sunrise: New Port, tel: 26610 26511/26610 44325

In the UK, it's well worth going through a consolidator or packager of medium-to-long-term car rental. Two particularly good ones are **Transhire**, tel: 0870/7898000, www.transhire.com, and **Autos Abroad**, tel: 0870/0667788, www.autosabroad.co.uk

There are ample petrol stations throughout Corfu. Parking in the capital is an endurance test; the only uncontrolled spaces tend to be out near the British Cemetery – otherwise resign yourself to using the fee area on the Spianádha, or at the Old Port.

HOURS AND HOLIDAYS

Business Hours

Government agencies are open weekdays 8am–2pm; banks 8am–2.30pm Monday to Thursday and 8am–2pm Friday; shop hours (which can vary by half an hour seasonally) are from around 9am–2pm and 5.30–8.30pm Tuesday, Thursday and Friday, and from 8.30am–2.30pm Monday, Wednesday and Saturday; department stores and supermarkets are open 8am–8pm, Monday to Friday and from 8am–6pm on Saturday. Call individual places of interest and museums for their opening hours (as far as possible these have been included in the itineraries section of this guide). Kiosks open very early and close very late throughout the main tourist season.

Public Holidays

All banks, government offices, shops and most sites close for the following: New Year's Day, 1 January; Epiphany, 6 January; First Monday in Lent, moveable; Greek Independence Day, 25 March; Good Friday, moveable; Greek Orthodox Easter, moveable; Easter Monday, moveable; Labour Day, 1 May; Pentecost (Whit Monday), moveable; Feast of the Dormition of the Virgin, 15 August; 'Ohi' Day, 28 October; Christmas Day, 25 December; Gathering of the Virgin's Entourage, 26 December; and, unofficially, St Spyrídhon's Days, 11 August and 12 December.

ACCOMMODATION

The best advice for first-time visitors is to stay in Kérkyra Town for the first part of your visit; then, after four or five days, relocate to a congenial beach resort or – taking things to remote extremes – to Paxí or even one of the Dhiapóndia islets. Like most of Greece, Corfu (except arguably for the town itself) offers great value for money accommodation-wise, and you shouldn't dismiss a luxury hotel out of hand; a price that would get you no more than a grim closet in London or New York will net you a superb bungalow with a view or a characterful room near the Spianádha.

In the following lists, € = inexpensive, €€ = moderate, €€€ = expensive; unless otherwise indicated, establishments are only open April to October.

It's wise to book well in advance, either direct (via fax or e-mail), or through a travel agent *(see page 96)*. There are numerous

Right: basic needs met here

rooms and apartments to rent on Corfu, but only local travel agents will know who is renting something attractive and reputable, year on year. You can always take the lazy way out and book a cheap-and-cheerful, all-inclusive beach holiday through a package operator in Britain, but you will usually find yourself restricted to the north coast between Sidhári and Kassiópi, and the far south around Benítses, Messongí, Ághios Yeórghios Argyrádhes or (shudder) Kávos.

Aharávi
St George's Bay Country Club Hotel
PO Box 40
Tel: 26630 63203/63225
Fax: 26630 63540
This cloister-like arrangement of stone bungalows and villas, surrounded by extensive gardens, is right on the endless beach at Aharávi. It caters primarily for German visitors and has a pool, tennis and an excellent beachfront restaurant (Prospero's, tel: 26630 63247, ext. 16), open for all meals.€€€

Dhafníla/Komméno
Hotel Nefeli
Tel: 26610 91033
Fax: 26610 90290
The pretty, salmon-pink Nefeli – 45 rooms housed in a lovely modern building – is located on the ritziest section of the east coast and shares some of the perks of nearby 4- and 5-star hotels: the Nefeli features balconies, spacious gardens, pool with a poolside bar, and great service.€€

Dhassiá
Grecotel Dafnila Bay Thalasso
PO Box 27
Tel: 26610 90321/90324
Fax: 26610 91026
Part of the respected Grecotel chain, renovated in 1999, this 260-room-and-bungalow complex caters for families. 11km (7 miles) from the capital, it is luxurious and facilities include multiple restaurants and bars, child care, thalassotherapy spa, fitness activities and a private beach. Half board. €€€

Érmones
Sunmarotel Ermones
Tel: 26610 94241
Fax: 26610 94248
e-mail: ermones@otenet.gr
Another of the island's premier hotels, this 600-bed hotel and bungalow complex 17km (10½ miles) from the capital is set above Érmones Bay. A téléferique plies between the clifftop and the beach, serving the bungalows arranged in tiers. The hotel has two restaurants, a health and fitness centre, tennis courts, sauna and jacuzzi, air-conditioning and sea views. Half-board included.€€€

Glyfádha/Pélekas
Menigos Resort
Tel: 26610 95074/94083
Fax: 26610 94933
e-mail: xenia_LTD@hotmail.com
Managed by Maximos Koulouris, this 700-bed/141-bungalow complex sprawls through gardens along the entire length of beautiful

Glyfádha Beach, some 20km (12 miles) from the capital. The self-catering bungalows, which are individually owned but let to visitors, are quickly snapped up, so you will need to fax Mr Koulouris well in advance to make your reservation.€€

Gouviá
Louis Corcyra Beach Hotel
Tel: 26610 90196
Fax: 26610 91591
e-mail: corcyra@sail.vacation.forthnet.gr
website: www.louishotels.com/greece/corfu/corfu.htm
Not far from Gouviá's excellent marina and located right on the beach, this 260-room member of the Louis hotel chain is 13km (8 miles) north of the capital. The hotel, spread over two main buildings, has in-house restaurants and bars, full air-conditioning and gorgeous public rooms. Leisure facilities include pools, tennis and squash courts.€€€

Molfetta Beach
Tel: 26610 91915/9
Fax: 26610 91919
Situated a stone's throw from the beach in busy little Gouviá, the 28-room Molfetta – modest but good value – is 7km (around 4 miles) from the capital. There's a good in-house restaurant, two bars, a disco – and a Sunday night Greek dancing demonstration.€

Kanóni
Corfu Holiday Palace
PO Box 124
Tel: 26610 36540
Fax: 26610 36551/45933
This high-rise, with 256 rooms, 14 suites and 35 bungalows, is all but within walking distance of Kérkyra, and has lovely views of Pontikoníssi. Impeccably managed, the hotel has two pools, a private beach, air-conditioning, health club, tennis, a watersports school, an in-house restaurant and the Kefi Bar – plus the casino, and free transfers to the Corfu Golf Club. Open all year.€€€

Kérkyra
Arhontiko
61 M. Athanasíou
Tel: 26610 37222

Fax: 26610 38294/20708
e-mail: belvenht@hol.gr
Under the same management as the Bella Venezia, this is another central hotel housed in a neoclassical mansion. There are 30 large rooms, some with adjoining sitting rooms, which makes the Arhontiko especially suitable for families. Renovated in 2000. Open all year.€€

Bella Venezia
4 N Zambéli Street
Tel: 26610 46500/44290
Fax: 26610 20708
e-mail: belvenht@hol.gr
website: www.kerkyra.net/bellavenezia/
Managed by Mr Theodore Ziniatis, this is a special place. Comprising 32 rooms in a neoclassical mansion at the south edge of the old town, this hotel has wonderful, personalised service, is open year round, and is convenient for everything. There is air-conditioning and an in-house bar, and you can take breakfast in the garden.€€

Cavalieri
4 Kapodhistriou
Tel: 26610 39041
Fax: 26610 39283
website: www.cavalieri-hotel.com
A-class hotel occupying a 17th-century building overlooking the Spianádha, the Albanian coast and the Paleó Froúrio. Frankly overpriced, with smallish rooms, but almost all of them have sea views from Venetian balconies, and the roof garden makes the place. Open all year.€€€

Corfu Palace
2 Dhimokratías, north end of Garítsa Bay
Tel: 26610 39485
Fax: 26610 31749
website: www.corfupalace.com
Kérkyra's town's only 'Lux' class establishment, this enjoys a high level of repeat clientele, including VIPs and foreign dignitaries, especially during May and September. They come for the 115 huge rooms (renovated in 1995) with marble tubs in the baths, the huge seawater pool, the big breakfasts at the generally excellent restaurant and the assiduous level of service. Open all year. €€€

Left: Nefeli Hotel

Konstantinoupolis
Zavitsianoú 11, Old Port
Tel: 26610 48716
Fax: 26610 48718
This 1862-dated building, the first ever built in town and for long a backpackers' dosshouse, has been lovingly restored in accordance with its vintage as a well-priced C-class hotel with sea and mountain views. On-site restaurant and heating, though no air conditioning. Open all year. €€

Komméno
Grecotel Corfu Imperial
Tel: 26610 91490
Fax: 26610 91881
website: www.grecotel.gr
Universally acknowledged as the best hotel on the island – and yet the staff is so personable and friendly that the place doesn't have that snobbishness one comes to expect from the perfect. The location, on the Komméno Peninsula, 10km (6 miles) from Kérkyra, is exquisite, the hotel is beautifully designed, and the restaurants, bars, shops, fitness club, watersport school, pools and private beaches all make the stiff rates worth it. Three grades of lodging: standard rooms, bungalows and a few super-luxe villas (the latter at around €800). €€€

Kondókali
Kontokali Bay
Tel: 26610 99000–2
Fax: 26610 91901
e-mail: kontobay@compulink.gr
website: www.medhotels.com
This hotel and bungalow complex with sea views is on the wooded Kondókali Peninsula, 6km (4 miles) from the capital. It's packed with amenities: sea views, elegant public rooms, marble baths, air-conditioning, mini-bars, three restaurants, a pool and two beaches. €€€

Liapádhes
Liapades Beach
Tel: 26630 41115/41370
Two smallish wings, not monopolised by tour groups, make up this amiable C-class hotel at one of the quieter beach resorts on the west-central coast. One restored old

building contains 28 standard rooms; the modern unit has 10 self-catering studios. €€

Nissáki
Falcon Travel
Tel: 26630 91318
Fax: 26630 91070
website: www.falcon-travel-corfu.com
British-owned travel agency that can arrange stays in either a dozen beach-side apartments in the area or two sensitively restored houses in the idyllic Mt Pandokrátor hamlet of Tritsí.€ apartments,€€ village houses.

Paleokastrítsa
Fundana Villas
4km before Paleokastrítsa
Tel: 26630 22532
A 17th-century Venetian farm-manor that's been converted into a 10-unit bungalow complex, with the old olive press as the main common area. Good for families (the units hold up to five people), with a pool and 8-ha (20-acre) setting near the north end of the lovely Rópa valley. Open Mar–Oct.€€

Odysseus
Tel: 26630 41209
Fax: 26630 41342
website: www.odysseushotel.gr
This reasonably priced, no frills family hotel 23km (14 miles) west of the capital is located just above the beach at Paleokastrítsa resort and is convenient for everything. Small but economical and well run, it has a pool and in-house restaurant.€€

Paxí
Paxi Beach
Gaïos
Tel: 26620 31211
Hillside bungalow complex leading down through trees to its own small pebble beach about 2km (1 mile) east of town.€€

Pithari Villas
Gaïos
Tel/Fax: 26620 32491
(in Athens tel: 01 681 7025)
Ms Vassiliki Malamas's Pithari is a wonderful place to stay. Only 50m (160ft) from the marina in the port of Gaïos, this accommodation comprises a villa, which

e-mail: sanders@otenet.gr
These 10, self-contained cottages share gracious public space, a pool and a delightful garden. Open all year and owned by Ms Val Androutsopoulou, the Casa Lucia sponsors New Age courses, classes, retreats and clinics *(see page 52)*. No credit cards.€€

Yialiskári
Yialiskari Palace Hotel
Tel: 26610 54401–2
Fax: 26610 54724
e-mail: rizosresorts@sympnia.com
Overlooking Yaliskari Bay, 15km (9 miles) from the capital, this member of the Rizos hotel chain has 230 rooms and suites, pool, tennis courts, sauna, and an in-house restaurant and bar.€€€

sleeps six, apartments for two and four guests, and a cottage for two, all furnished with antiques and surrounded by lush gardens.€€

Pélekas
Levant
Tel: 26610 94230
Fax: 26610 94115
website: www.levant-hotel.com
Smallish A-class hotel in neoclassical style taking full advantage of this village's famous views over the Ionian and the lush countryside. Swimming pool and good breakfasts to make up for a lack of beachside setting. Unusually for a rural hotel, it's open until November.€€

Perouládhes
Villa de Loulia
Tel/Fax: 26630 95394
This tiny (nine rooms/suites) neoclassical jewel is 34km (21 miles) from the capital, less than 500m (¼ mile) from Longás Beach beyond the Canal d'Amour. The building, which dates from 1803, is owned/managed by Ms Loukia Mataranga, and pricy creature comforts abound: antique furnishings, orthopaedic mattresses, internet service, and flowers and fruit upon arrival.€€€

Sgómbou
Casa Lucia
Tel: 26610 91419
Fax: 26610 91732

HEALTH & EMERGENCIES

Hygiene/General Health
Tap water is safe to drink in the Ionian islands, but bottled water – especially the two Greek sparkling brands, Sariza and Souroti – tastes much better.

Sun and heat stroke, and the ill effects of too much alcohol (or too much olive oil) consumed while on holiday are the most common health challenges faced by visitors. However, scooter and motorbike mishaps are also a very real hazard on Corfu: only ride any two-wheeler here if you are a proficient motorcyclist, and always wear protective clothing, strong shoes and a helmet, even though the weather might be stifling. Otherwise, hire a car instead.

Be aware that there are some unfriendly, if rarely encountered, creatures on the island. Poisonous vipers really do want to get out of your way before you tread on them, but on rare occasions they don't, so wear sensible walking boots and watch your step. To protect against sea urchins, swim in purpose-made slippers (and wear goggles or a mask so you can spot them); footwear should also take care of the threat from the bottom-dwelling weever fish *(dhrákena)*, whose poisonous spines contain a potentially lethal toxin. If precautions fail, try to neutralise the poison by applying hot water to the affected site while waiting for a doctor.

Above: a police officer ready to assist

Note: flying within 24 hours of scuba diving can bring on nitrogen embolism, requiring an emergency transfer to a decompression chamber.

Pharmacies

Pharmacies/chemists *(farmakía)* abound on Corfu, but I have two favourites in Kérkyra: Mrs Sylvaine Kavadas Pharmacy, 66 Evgheníou Voulgáreos Street, tel: 26610 25378; and K Grammenandi and N Trivizas Pharmacy/Homeopathics, 76 Evgheníou Voulgáreos Street, tel: 26610 30100.

Medical/Dental Services

Depending on the nature of your dental or health needs, either consult your hotel concierge for a list of accredited and trusted physicians and dentists; phone the Tourist Police; or go by taxi or ambulance to Corfu General Hospital *(Yenikó Nosokomío Kérkyras)*, where the emergency room staff will make a diagnosis. **Corfu General Hospital:** Corner Andreadhí and Konstandá streets, near San Rocco, tel: 26610 36044/88200.

Emergency Telephone Numbers

Ambulance: tel: 166 or 26610 39403
Fire: tel: 26610 199/191
Police: tel: 100 (see also regional numbers below)
Tourist Police: 4 Samartzí Street, San Rocco Square, Kérkyra; tel: 26610 30265
Traffic Police: tel: 26610 39294
Breakdowns: ELPA, tel: 26610 39504;
Express Service, tel: 154 or 26610 44244. The local number generally works better.
Regional Police Numbers
Ághios Matthéos, tel: 26610 75113
Argyrádhes, tel: 26620 51422
Benítses, tel: 26610 72222
Gaïos, Paxí, tel: 26620 32222
Karousádhes, tel: 26630 31222
Kastelláni, tel: 26610 54222
Lefkími, tel: 26620 22222
Magouládhes, tel: 26630 95222
Othoní, Dhiapóndia islets, tel: 26630 71592
Paleokastrítsa, tel: 26630 41203
Skriperó, tel: 26630 22222
Yiannádes, tel: 26610 51222
Yimári, tel: 26630 91261
Ýpsos, tel: 26610 93204

COMMUNICATION & NEWS

Postal Services

The main Post Office *(Tahydhromío)* in Kérkyra is located at the corner of Alexándhras Avenue and Rizospáston Vouleftón Street (tel: 26610 25544; Mon–Fri 7.30am–2pm, also some evening hours, check for times). Note: upon entering, be sure to take a number from an automated machine and wait your turn.

Yellow post boxes for ordinary mail are situated all over the island; red boxes are for express mail. Post offices in Greece have specific windows for regular post and stamps *(grammatósima)*, sending parcels, *post restante* and girobank transactions.

Telephones

There are numerous phone boxes across the island, usually stationed at the noisiest intersections, which take OTE (Greek telecom) phone cards; these are available at kiosks *(períptera)*, newsagents and other sorts of shops in several denominations, and are the cheapest way of making calls. If you're not going to be around long enough to get full use out of a card, seek out the growing number of countertop pay-phones which take 5-, 10- and 20-cent coins, or find one of the few remaining metered phones at a kiosk (where you pay after making the call). However, none of these types of phones can be rung back, which makes it problematic for people to stay in touch with you. The best solution for that is to carry a mobile phone. Almost all European providers have roaming agreements with at least one of the three mobile networks trading in Greece. In any event, avoid using hotel room phones, at least for outgoing calls – the surcharges can run up to four times the basic OTE rate.

To make international calls, dial 00, followed by the country code, the area code (omitting the initial 0 except for Italy) then the number.

Directory Enquiries: tel: 131
International Directory Enquiries: tel: 161
Internet Access
See the listings of internet cafés in Nightlife chapter, pages 78–9.

Media

Corfu supports a huge number of local newspapers and broadcasting stations, but visitors will probably confine themselves to the major television channels received at their hotels, and 'graze' among the radio stations picked up in their hire cars. Day-later foreign press is readily available throughout the island at the most unlikely shops (*see address on page 71* for a Kérkyra newsagent).

The Corfiot: Corfu's English Language Monthly Magazine (PO Box 445, tel: 26610 52833; www.corfunews.net) is edited by the local author and leader of walks and excursions *extraordinaire*, Ms Hilary Whitton Païpeti, and is packed with useful information.

USEFUL INFORMATION

Visitors with Disabilities

Greece – and Corfu is no exception – is a challenge and a half for visitors with disabilities. Accommodation, transport, sites, toilets – nothing is truly disabled-friendly the length and breadth of the country (this should change due to EU directives, but this will take time). Kérkyra itself, so readily accessible from the airport by taxi, and not crisscrossed with flights of steps, is far easier to negotiate than, say, Athens or the Cyclades.

Telephone or fax a trusted travel agent recommended on page 96 and discuss your special needs with them before planning your trip. Ms Aperghi and Mr Paniperis should then be able to map out accommodation, excursions and transport to fit your requirements.

Children

Young visitors are universally welcomed on the island. Most of the itineraries in this guide have been designed with travellers of all ages and abilities in mind, and all of the accommodation has been vetted with an eye to young people's needs. Corfu is much better prepared for families with young children than some of the more sophisticated islands further south, though you may perhaps choose not to take your youngsters to the resort of Kávos, or the nudist beach at Myrtiótissa.

THE GREEK LANGUAGE

Greek is a phonetic language. There are some combinations of vowels and consonants which customarily stand for certain sounds and some slight pronunciation changes determined by which letter follows but, generally, sounds are pronounced as they are written, without additions or omissions.

If you touch down in Athens en route to Corfu, you will find that most Athenians have some knowledge of English, and most Greeks are delighted to find a visitor making stabs at speaking Greek. (The Greeks do not ridicule you for making mistakes but will often correct you: they themselves have a hard time with Greek spelling and the complicated Greek grammar.) Whatever you can accomplish, guide book in hand, will be rewarded.

In addition to pronouncing each letter, you should remember that stress plays a vital role in Modern Greek. When you learn a Greek word, learn where the stress falls at the same time. Each Greek word has a single main stress (marked in the following vocabulary list with an accent).

Greek is an inflected language and noun and adjective endings change according to

Above: travelling with children

Ναός Αντιβουνιώτισσας
Βυζαντινό Μουσείο
Church of the Antivouniotissa
Byzantine Museum

Πύλη Αγίου Νικολάου
Gate of Ayios Nikolaos

gender, number and case. Case endings and the conjugation of Greek verbs are, unfortunately, beyond the scope of a guide book.

The Greek Alphabet

Cap.	l.c.	Value	Name
Α	α	a in father	alfa
Β	β	v in visa	vita
Γ	γ	ghama gh when medial, y when initial	
Δ	δ	th in then	delta
Ε	ε	e in let	epsilon
Ζ	ζ	z in zebra	zita
Η	η	i in ski	ita
Θ	θ	th in theory	thita
Ι	ι	i in ski	yota
Κ	κ	k in king	kapa
Λ	λ	l in million	lamda
Μ	μ	m in mouse	mi
Ν	ν	n in no	ni
Ξ	ξ	x as in box	ksi
Ο	ο	o in oh	omikron
Π	π	p in pebble	pi
Ρ	ρ	r in raisin	ro
Σ	σ	s in sun, except pronounced z before g & m sounds	sigma
Τ	τ	t in trireme	taf
Ε	ε	y in clearly	ipsilon
Φ	φ	f in favour	fi
Χ	χ	h in help	hi
Ψ	ψ	ps in copse	psi
Ω	ω	o in oh	omega

Dipthongs

Type	Value
αι	e in hey
αυ	av or af in avert or after
ει	i in ski
ευ	ev or ef
οι	i in ski
ου	oo in poor

Double consonants

μπ	b at beginnings of words; mb in the middle of words
ντ	d at beginnings of words; nd in the middle of words
τζ	dz as in adze
γγ, γκ	g at the beginnings of words; ng in the middle of words

Vocabulary

Note: The following words are broken into syllables (not separate words), the stressed syllable marked with an accent. Greeks don't accent one-syllable words, but we do for clarity and learning purposes. Pronounce *e* as in pet; *a* as in father; *i* as in ski; *o* as in oh; *u* as in tune.

Numbers

Note: many foods and drinks take the feminine form of 'one' *(mí-a)*.

one *é-na* (neuter)/*é-nas* (masc.)/*mí-a* (fem.)
two *dhýo*
three *trí-a* (neuter)/*tris* (masc. and fem.)
four *té-sse-ra, tésseres* (masc. and fem.)
five *pén-de*
six *éxi*
seven *ep-tá/eftá*
eight *ok-tó*
nine *e-né-a/enyá*
ten *dhéka*
eleven *éndheka*
twelve *dhódheka*
thirteen *dhe-ka-trí-a/dhe-ka-trís*
fourteen *dhe-ka-té-sse-ra/dhékatésseres*
etc. until twenty
twenty *í-ko-si*
thirty *tri-án-da*
forty *sa-rán-da*
fifty *pe-nín-da*
sixty *exínda*
seventy *ev-dho-mín-da*
eighty *og-dhón-da*
ninety *e-ne-nín-da*
one hundred *e-ka-tó*
two hundred *dhi-a-kó-si-a* (neuter)
three hundred *tri-a-kó-si-a* (neuter)
four hundred *te-tra-kó-si-a* (neuter)
one thousand *hí-lia* (neuter)

Above: the way ahead

Note: Since the word for euro *(evró)* is neuter and undeclined, a number preceding this noun will also be neuter. Thus, *téssera evró*, for 4 euros.

Days of the Week
Monday *Dhef-té-ra*
Tuesday *Trí-ti*
Wednesday *Te-tár-ti*
Thursday *Pém-pti*
Friday *Pa-ras-ke-ví*
Saturday *Sá-vva-to*
Sunday *Ky-ri-a-kí*
yesterday *kthes*
today *sí-me-ra*
tomorrow *á-vri-o*

Greetings
Hello *yiá sas* (plural/polite)/*yiá sou* (sing./familiar) *yiá* (abbreviated)
Good day *ka-li mé-ra*
Good evening *ka-lí spé-ra*
Good night *kalí ník-ta*
Welcome *ka-lós íl-tha-te*
Good luck *ka-lí týhi*
How are you? *Ti ká-ne-te?* (plural/polite)/*Ti ká-nis?* (singular/familiar)
fine (in response) *ka-lá*
pleased to meet you *há-ri-ka*

Getting Around
yes *né*
no *ó-hi*
okay *en dá-x-i*
thank you *ef-ha-ris-tó*
excuse me *sig-nó-mi*
It doesn't matter *dhen pirázi*
It's nothing *tí-po-ta*
certainly/polite yes *má-li-sta*
Can I..? *Bo-ró na..?*
When? *Pó-te?*
Where is..? *Poú í-n-e..?*
Do you speak English? *Mi-lá-te an-gli-ká?*
Do you understand? *Ka-ta-la-vé-ne-te?*
What time is it? *Ti ó-ra í-ne?*
What time will it leave? *Ti ó-ra tha fýghi?*
I don't *dhén* (plus verb)
I want *thé-lo*
I have *é-ho*
here/there *e-dhó/e-kí*
near/far *kon-dá/ma-kry-á*
small/large *mi-kró/me-gá-lo*

quickly *grí-go-ra*
slowly *ar-gá*
good/bad *ka-ló/ka-kó*
warm/cold *zes-tó/krý-o*
bus *le-o-for-í-o*
boat *ka-rá-vi, va-pó-ri*
hydrofoil *dhelfíni*
scooter *papáki*
motorcycle *motosikléta*
bicycle *podhílato*
ticket *i-si-tí-ri-o*
road/street *dhró-mos/o-dhós*
beach *pa-ra-lí-a*
sea *thá-la-ssa*
church *e-kli-sí-a*
ancient ruin *ar-hé-a*
centre *kén-dro*
square *pla-tí-a*

Hotels
hotel *xe-no-dho-hí-o*
Do you have a room? *É-he-te é-na dho-má-ti-o?*
bed *kre-vá-ti*
shower with hot water *doúz mé zes-tó neró*
key *kli-dhí*
toilet *toua-lé-ta*
women's *yi-ne-kón*
men's *án-dron*

Shopping
store *ma-ga-zí*
kiosk *pe-ríp-te-ro*
open/shut *a-nik-tó/klis-tó*
post office *ta-hy-dhro-mí-o*
stamp *gra-ma-tó-simo*
letter *grám-ma*
envelope *fá-ke-lo*
telephone *ti-lé-fo-no*
bank *trá-pe-za*
marketplace *a-go-rá*
Have you..? *É-he-te..?*
Is there..? *É-hi..?*
How much does it cost? *Pó-so ká-ni?*
It's (too) expensive *Í-ne (po-lý) a-kri-vó*
How many? *Pó-sa?*

Emergencies
doctor *yia-trós*
hospital *no-so-ko-mí-o*
pharmacy *far-ma-kí-o*
police *as-ty-no-mí-a*
station *stath-mós*

USEFUL ADDRESSES

Tourist Offices

EOT, or the Hellenic Tourist Organisation of Greece (corner of Rizospáston Vouleftón and Polylá streets, Kérkyra; tel: 26610 37520/37638; Mon–Fri 8am–2pm)

Travel Agencies

Aperghi Travel and Tourism
Dhimokratías Avenue and 1 I Polylá Street
Tel: 26610 48713–14
Fax: 26610 48715
e-mail: aperghi@travelling.gr
website: www.travelling.gr/aperghi
Ms Anna S Aperghi is is a long-time tourism professional and her service is personalised, prompt and cordial. Fax or e-mail her in advance to arrange accommodation. An attractive new option is a 7- or 14-day tour based on the new Corfu Trail.

Corfu Infotravel LTD
14 Ethnikís Antistásseos Street
New Port
Kérkyra
Tel: 26610 41550/25933/25792;
Fax: 26610 23829
e-mail: infotravel@ker.forthnet.gr
Paxiot Mr Dimitris Paniperis has a large, modern travel agency near the quays and will be happy to arrange for all your travel needs.

Planos Tours
Lákka, Paxí
Tel: 26620 31744
Fax: 26620 31010
One of two agencies in this little port, efficiently handling everything from basic rooms to luxurious villas, as well as all travel arrangements back to Corfu or the mainland.

FURTHER READING

A few of these books are now rare or even antiquarian, but don't give up – most can be found at a reasonable price on not only on Amazon (.co.uk and .com), but also Barnes & Noble (www.bn.com) and www.abe.com
Captain Correlli's Mandolin by Louis de Bernières (Mandarin/Vintage). Though set on nearby Kefalloniá, this war-and-romance epic is a distillation of all things Ionian. Don't judge it by the truly forgettable 2001 movie starring Nicholas Cage and Penelope Cruz; it's a complex and occasionally dark work which caused considerable controversy in Greece for its less-than-flattering portrayal of the World War II resistance movement.
Corfu: The Garden Isle, edited by Spiro Flamburiari and Frank Giles (John Murray, now o/p). Beautifully illustrated coffee-table book that's a native son's labour of informed love. Fairly easy to find on Amazon, or in better Kérkyra hotels.
Edward Lear: The Corfu Years, edited and introduced by Philip Sherrard (Denise Harvey, UK & Greece). The late philhellenic scholar Sherrard produced an engaging portrait of watercolourist, humourist and 19th-century Balkan traveller Lear in this welcome reissue; the original is expensive antiquarian stock.
Ionia Nissia: Sta Ihni tou Odhyssea/The Ionian Islands: In the Tracks of Odysseus. Photographs by Nikos Dhessylas, historical essay (Greek-English) by Nikos Moskhonas (Synolo Publications, Greece). Local photographer Dhessylas' stunning portfolio is a 'must' souvenir purchase.
In the Footsteps of Lawrence Durrell and Gerald Durrell in Corfu (1935–39): A Modern Guidebook by Hilary Whitton Païpeti (Hermes Press, Corfu). Easily available at island bookshops.
Prospero's Cell: A Guide to the Landscape and Manners of the Island of Corcyra (Faber & Faber/Marlowe & Co). First penned in 1960 and in print once again, this nostalgic survey of characters and customs from the 1930s is all-but-mandatory pre-visit reading.
Prospero's Kitchen: Mediterranean Cooking of the Ionian Islands from Corfu to Kythera (Pedestrian Publications, Corfu & UK/M Evans & Co). An amalgam of history, local lore and heirloom recipes; easy to find on the island, best bought overseas through websites.
The Second Book of Corfu Walks: The Road to Old Corfu (Hermes Press, Corfu) and *The Companion Guide to the Corfu Trail* (Pedestrian Productions, Corfu & UK). Finely detailed walks across the island by Hilary Whitton Païpeti; the Corfu Trail is a 2001-inaugurated, long-distance route from one end of the island to the other. Both are easily available on Corfu, or through Amazon.

Right: clear waters

credits

ACKNOWLEDGEMENTS

Photography	**Elizabeth Boleman-Herring** *and*
10, 11, 12, 13,	**AKG Photo**
14	**Byzantine Museum**
15	**Topham Picturepoint**
Cover	**Robert Harding**
Back Cover	**Elizabeth Boleman-Herring**
23, 24t&b, 32, 37, 45, 72, 85	**Phil Wood/Apa Publications**
Cartography	**Berndtson & Berndtson**

The author would like to thank Anna Aperghi, Ruth Bossard, Nella Pantazi, Paris, Jennifer and Eleonora Raftopoulos, Anita Vassilakopoulou, Ioannis Vlachos, and the owners, management and staff of the Bella Venezia Hotel and the Corfu Holiday Palace Hotel. Thanks, also, to all the wonderful people of Corfu who made this book such a pleasure to research, photograph and write.

© APA Publications GmbH & Co. Verlag KG Singapore Branch, Singapore

INSIGHT
Pocket Guides

The travel guides that replace a tour guide – now better than ever with more listings and a fresh new design

Insight Pocket Guides pioneered a new approach to guidebooks, introducing the concept of the authors as "local hosts" who would provide readers with personal recommendations, just as they would give honest advice to a friend who came to stay. They also included a full-size pull-out map.

Now, to cope with the needs of the 21st century, new editions in this growing series are being given a new look to make them more practical to use, and restaurant and hotel listings have been greatly expanded.

INSIGHT GUIDES

The world's largest collection of visual travel guides

Now in association with

Discovery CHANNEL

Also from Insight Guides...

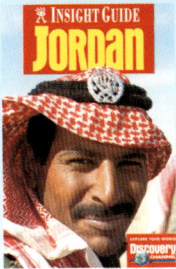

Insight Guides is the classic series, providing the complete picture with expert and informative text and stunning photography. Each book is an ideal travel planner, a reliable on-the-spot companion – and a superb visual souvenir of a trip. 193 titles.

Insight Maps are designed to complement the guidebooks. They provide full mapping of major destinations, and their laminated finish gives them ease of use and durability. 100 titles.

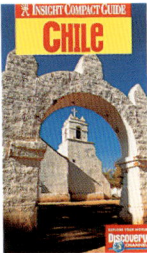

Insight Compact Guides are handy reference books, modestly priced yet comprehensive. The text, pictures and maps are all cross-referenced, making them ideal books to consult while seeing the sights. 127 titles.

INSIGHT POCKET GUIDE TITLES

Aegean Islands
Algarve
Alsace
Amsterdam
Athens
Atlanta
Bahamas
Baja Peninsula
Bali
Bali Bird Walks
Bangkok
Barbados
Barcelona
Bavaria
Beijing
Berlin
Bermuda
Bhutan
Boston
Brisbane & the
  Gold Coast
British Columbia
Brittany
Brussels
Budapest
California,
  Northern

Canton
Cape Town
Chiang Mai
Chicago
Corfu
Corsica
Costa Blanca
Costa Brava
Costa del Sol
Costa Rica
Crete
Croatia
Denmark
Dubai
Fiji Islands
Florence
Florida
Florida Keys
French Riviera
  (Côte d'Azur)
Gran Canaria
Hawaii
Hong Kong
Hungary
Ibiza
Ireland
Ireland's Southwest

Israel
Istanbul
Jakarta
Jamaica
Kathmandu Bikes
  & Hikes
Kenya
Kraków
Kuala Lumpur
Lisbon
Loire Valley
London
Los Angeles
Macau
Madrid
Malacca
Maldives
Mallorca
Malta
Manila
Melbourne
Mexico City
Miami
Montreal
Morocco
Moscow
Munich

Nepal
New Delhi
New Orleans
New York City
New Zealand
Oslo and Bergen
Paris
Penang
Perth
Phuket
Prague
Provence
Puerto Rico
Quebec
Rhodes
Rome
Sabah
St. Petersburg
San Diego
San Francisco
Sarawak
Sardinia
Scotland
Seville, Cordoba &
  Granada
Seychelles
Sicily

Sikkim
Singapore
Southeast England
Southern Spain
Sri Lanka
Stockholm
Switzerland
Sydney
Tenerife
Thailand
Tibet
Toronto
Tunisia
Turkish Coast
Tuscany
Venice
Vienna
Vietnam
Yogjakarta
Yucatán Peninsula

INDEX